Isabel Holm.

181

TWO HUNDRED AND FIFTY YEARS
OF SCOTTISH EDUCATION 1696-1946

TWO HUNDRED AND FIFTY YEARS OF SCOTTISH EDUCATION

1696-1946

BY

H. M. KNOX, M.A., B.ED., PH.D.

PROFESSOR OF EDUCATION, QUEEN'S UNIVERSITY, BELFAST
SOMETIME LECTURER IN EDUCATION, UNIVERSITY OF ST. ANDREWS

OLIVER AND BOYD
EDINBURGH: TWEEDDALE COURT
LONDON: 98 GREAT RUSSELL STREET, W.C.

FIRST PUBLISHED 1953

PRINTED IN GREAT BRITAIN BY
ROBERT CUNNINGHAM AND SONS LTD., ALVA
FOR OLIVER AND BOYD LTD., EDINBURGH

CONTENTS

CHAPTER | PAGE

Foreword ix

Introduction xi

Part I The Eighteenth Century

I. Education in the Eighteenth Century 3

Early attempts at educational legislation — Act for Settling of Schools — the S.S.P.C.K. — burgh schools — spinning schools — academies — the universities — professional training

Part II The First Half of the Nineteenth Century

II. Elementary Education to 1864 23

Parochial Schoolmasters Act — side schools — sessional schools — *quoad sacra* parishes — assembly schools — Treasury grants — parliamentary schools — Committee of Council on Education — Free Church schools — Owen and Stow — Science and Art Department — the Education Department — Newcastle Commission — Parochial and Burgh Schoolmasters Act — 'Payment by Results'

III. Higher Education before 1860 37

(*a*) The Schools: administrative confusion — mixed burgh and parochial schools — endowed and proprietary schools — uncertainty of organization and curriculum — technical education; (*b*) The Universities: Rosebery Commission — proposal for university at Dumfries — abolition of tests — university reform

Part III The Middle of the Century

IV. The Education Act of 1872 55

Argyll Commission — Education Act of 1872 — Scotch Education Department — Board of Education for Scotland — school boards — compulsory attendance — rate-aid — first Scotch code — specific subjects

V. SECONDARY EDUCATION 1861-1878 69

Argyll Commission on burgh schools — endowed 'hospitals' — Endowed Institutions Act of 1869 — higher class public schools — Colebrooke Commission on endowments — Endowed Institutions Act of 1878

VI. THE UNIVERSITIES FROM 1858 TO 1889 86

Effects of the Universities Act of 1858 — work of executive commission — reform of graduation system — new degrees in science and law — Inglis Commission — foundation of Dundee University College

PART IV THE LATTER PART OF THE CENTURY

VII. ELEMENTARY EDUCATION 1873-1903 107

Report on 'specific subjects' — Education Act of 1883 — reorganization of the Department — Parker Committee — establishment of county councils — free elementary education — the Merit Certificate — Advanced Departments and Higher Grade Schools — the Intermediate Certificate — Education Act of 1901 — institution of the qualifying examination — Supplementary Courses

VIII. SECONDARY EDUCATION 1878-1908 121

Educational Endowments Act of 1882 — education of girls — Technical Schools Act of 1887 — institution of the Leaving Certificate — grants for technical and secondary education — secondary education committees — organized science schools — modifications of Leaving Certificate examination

IX. TEACHER TRAINING BEFORE 1906 139

David Stow and the Glasgow Educational Society — The Normal and Sessional School of Edinburgh — effect of the Disruption — pupil-teacher system — Queen's Scholars — combined training — chairs of education — postgraduate diplomas — Queen's Students — establishment of Provincial Committees

X. THE UNIVERSITIES SINCE 1889 153

Universities Act of 1889 — executive commission — incorporation of Dundee University College — higher education of women — institution of preliminary examinations — further reform of graduation system — admission of lecturers — Carnegie Trust — establishment of University Grants Committee — Scottish Universities Entrance Board — Acts of 1922 and 1932

PART V THE TWENTIETH CENTURY

XI. THE LEGISLATION OF 1908 AND 1918 — 175

Handicapped children — Education Act of 1908 — teachers' superannuation — Education (Scotland) Fund — industrial and reformatory schools — Education Act of 1918—county education authorities — settlement of the 'religious question' — devolution of administration — Local Government Act of 1929

XII. TEACHER TRAINING SINCE 1906 — 193

Establishment of training centres — regulations of 1906 — junior student system — degrees in education — National Committee for the Training of Teachers — regulations of 1924 and 1931 — 'emergency scheme' — teachers' terms of service — Educational Institute of Scotland — security of tenure

XIII. DEVELOPMENTS BETWEEN 1918 AND 1939 — 208

Post-primary reorganization of 1923 — abolition of Merit and Intermediate Certificates — Advanced Divisions — Day School Certificates — the 'clean cut' — Educational Endowments Act of 1928 — Scottish Council for Research in Education — approved schools — Education Act of 1936 — secondary education for all

XIV. THE PRESENT POSITION — 224

The impact of war — the Youth Service — educational reconstruction — Education Act of 1945 — consolidating Act of 1946 — Scottish Education Department — the inspectorate — functions of central and local authorities — 'direct-grant' schools — central institutions — technical and adult education — the Scottish tradition

BIBLIOGRAPHY — 243

INDEX — 247

FOREWORD

THIS WORK was completed in May 1951 while I was lecturer in education at the University of St. Andrews. Its appearance has been considerably delayed because of difficulties of publication in these days of prohibitive costs. That it has appeared at all is entirely due to the generosity of the Carnegie Trust for the Universities of Scotland in making available a grant of money and to the public-spiritedness of my publishers in deliberately undertaking a calculated risk on a work of necessarily limited appeal.

H. M. K.

Queen's University
Belfast
February 1953

INTRODUCTION

EDUCATIONALLY, Scotland has been described as the happy woman who has no history, but this surely does not imply an insensitiveness to her long educational tradition. Yet the complete dearth of up-to-date textbooks on the subject would appear to warrant such a view, for the most recent contribution to the general history of Scottish education is Alexander Morgan's *Rise and Progress of Scottish Education*, published in 1927 and now long out of print. Since that time several valuable works on English education have made their appearance, notably J. W. Adamson's *English Education*, 1789-1902 in 1930, Frank Smith's *History of English Elementary Education*, 1760-1902 in 1931 and H. C. Barnard's *Short History of English Education*, 1760-1944 in 1947, while the only general account of the Scottish system available at the present time consists of two chapters in S. J. Curtis's *History of Education in Great Britain* (1948). Mention must, of course, also be made of a number of regional and specialist monographs among the publications of the Scottish Council for Research in Education, and of N. A. Wade's excellent account of post-primary education in Scottish primary schools between 1872 and 1936, but there is manifestly a need for something of a more general character to supplement these. The aim of the present volume is to supply a concise account of the development of the statutory system from the time of the first relatively effective enactment on the subject to the passing of the comprehensive education act of 1946. For this purpose the diligent researches of James Grant, Graham Balfour, John Kerr and John Strong are indispensable material.

It must be admitted at the outset that the usual historical treatment of dealing *pari passu* with each separate stage in the educational system is not particularly appropriate to Scottish education, for not only have the distinctive stages been less sharply demarcated than elsewhere but the crucial points in the development of each stage have not necessarily coincided chronologically. Balfour illustrates this by remarking that 'the characteristic of Scotch education was that no one grade was entirely separate from another. Nearly all the schools were in some measure both elementary and secondary'. In more modern days Lord Eustace Percy amplifies this statement with the observation that 'no definite statutory distinction was drawn between the elementary and the secondary school, and the practical distinction tended to be, not between elementary and secondary schools, but between pupils doing elementary and secondary work in any school' (*Yearbook of Education*, 1934). Even the term 'elementary school', though frequently employed in official reports of the nineteenth century, has never been favoured in connection with Scottish education, for it has been held to imply a difference in kind, as well as degree, in educational provision. Nevertheless, for the sake of convenience the conventional method of treatment of subject matter and the traditional terminology have been adopted in the present instance, although with some reserve.

Finally, it may be well to offer some apology for the arbitrary choice of starting-point. The roots of Scottish popular education undoubtedly go deep into history and no picture of it can claim to be complete which merely takes up the threads at an externally convenient point. The 'Act for Settling of Schools' was only the culmination point of a number of earlier measures directed towards the same end, and the 'blue-print' of the present Scottish system is undoubtedly to be found as early as 1560 in the celebrated chapter of the First Book of Discipline dealing with schools and universities. Nearly all the progress achieved since then has been a gradual approximation to the ideals expressed in that document. But the turbulent state of the country from the time of the Reformation to the Union of the Crowns in 1603 and the subsequent ecclesiastical upheavals of the seventeenth century necessarily prevented any real educational development. It was only after the final settlement of the question of church government in favour of presbyterianism in 1690 and the Union of the Parliaments in 1707 with its consequent, though long delayed, increase in national prosperity that a measure of attention to the country's educational problems became a practical proposition. Then followed the Industrial Revolution with its widespread redistribution of population and the necessity for an enormous expansion of the educational services, an expansion which has continued unchecked until the present day. It seems possible, however, that the provisions of the act of 1946 mark the limit of what is attainable under our present economic system.

PART I

THE EIGHTEENTH CENTURY

CHAPTER I

EDUCATION IN THE EIGHTEENTH CENTURY

THE Act for Settling of Schools passed by the Scottish parliament in the year 1696 has frequently been referred to as the Magna Charta of Scottish education, realizing as it did (however imperfectly) the modest ideal of a school in every parish, and it serves as a convenient starting-point for the study of educational developments in Scotland during the modern period. It is only right to point out, however, that this important statute represented the culmination of a number of previous attempts to achieve the same object, rendered abortive by the political unrest of the seventeenth century. The earliest recorded endeavour to establish a parochial system of schools in the country seems to have been an act of the Scottish Privy Council of James VI, dated at Edinburgh on the 10th of December 1616 and expressing the King's anxiety that the true religion should be advanced and established in all parts of the kingdom.

It was stated in the preamble that to this end the youth should be trained up in civility, godliness, knowledge and learning, and that the common English tongue should universally replace the Irish [*sic*] language as one of the principal causes for the continuance of barbarity and incivility amongst the inhabitants of the highlands and islands. Since no more effective means of achieving this happy result could be devised than the establishment of schools in which young people might be taught at least to read and write, and be catechized and instructed in the grounds of religion, it was enacted that in every parish of the kingdom where the means existed a school should be established, and a fit person appointed to take charge of it, at the expense of the parishioners, according to the resources of the parish as estimated by a survey carried out by the bishop of the diocese. Every bishop was accordingly instructed to reach an agreement with the people of each parish in his diocese as to the best means of establishing such a school, and to refer any difficulty that might arise in the matter to the Lords of the Privy Council of Scotland.

The legality, as distinct from the effectiveness, of this procedure might perhaps be challenged, but some sixteen and a half years later an act of the Scottish parliament was passed, on 28th June 1633, ratifying the act of Privy Council anent Plantation of Schools. In addition, the bishop was authorized with the consent of the heritors and a majority of the parishioners (or indeed without the consent of the former should they refuse to appear) to set down and 'stent' upon the worth of every plough and husband land for the purpose of establishing and maintaining such schools. In cases of grievance a right of appeal to the Privy Council was granted. Comparatively little seems to have come of this well-meant piece of legislation, however, for barely thirteen years later the celebrated St. Andrews parliament deemed it necessary to promulgate another act in more explicit terms. This was the Act for Founding of Schools in every parish, passed on 2nd February 1646, ordaining that a school should be founded and a schoolmaster appointed in every parish not already provided for. A change in ecclesiastical government is indicated by the fact that on this occasion the act was to be implemented by the presbytery and no longer by the bishop of a diocese.

The heritors of every parish were instructed to meet together for the purpose of providing a commodious house for the school and compounding a salary for the schoolmaster of not less than 100 merks and not more than 200 merks (a range of between £5 11/1½ and £11 2/3) per annum, payable twice yearly. They were to set down a 'stent' (assessment) on everyone's rent of stock and 'teind' (tithe) in the parish proportional to its worth, for the purpose of maintaining the school and paying the master's salary, and in cases of failure to reach agreement the presbytery was to nominate twelve honest men from within its bounds to enforce the provisions of the act. The great weakness of this procedure lay, of course, in the fact that any suitable candidates for this task were more than likely to be heritors themselves and therefore could not be impartial judges of the law they were expected to implement. In any case, the measure, enlightened though it was, had the misfortune to originate from a parliament in revolt against its monarch, and at the Restoration it shared the fate of many more contumacious contemporaries. For on 28th March 1661 the Scottish parliament, in chastened mood, passed a rescissory act rescinding and annulling the acts of the 'pretended parliaments' of 1640, '41, '44, '45, '46, '47 and '48. This left the educational position the same as it had been in 1633, and to clarify the somewhat confused situation it was considered advisable to pass yet another act, largely re-enacting the provisions of the statute of 1646.

The Act for Settling of Schools, of 9th October 1696, once more decreed that in every parish not already provided for a school should be established and a schoolmaster appointed on the advice of the heritors and minister of the parish. Again the heritors were required to provide a commodious house for the school and settle a salary for the schoolmaster within the range of 100 to 200 merks, payable in equal portions at Whitsunday and Martinmas. As before, it was to be compounded on each heritor's valued rent within the parish, but on this occasion relief of half his share of the cost of settling and maintaining the school and paying the master's salary was sanctioned by passing it on to his tenants. To this precedent is attributed the present Scottish custom of levying local rates divided between owners and occupiers of property. In cases of disagreement the presbytery was given leave to apply to the Commissioners of Supply for the county, responsible for assessing the land-tax, any five of whom might, like the twelve honest men of fifty years earlier, see to the business of establishing a school and settling the schoolmaster's salary. For the same reason as before, however, the machinery of putting the law into effect was vitiated by the procedure of relying on officers who were in all probability heritors themselves. In consequence, it is hardly surprising that in many cases nothing was done to provide either a schoolhouse or a salary for a teacher, and, as H. G. Graham remarks, 'never was there a wiser law, and never was a law more studiously disregarded'. The removal of the legislature from Edinburgh to London at the Treaty of Union in 1707, only eleven years after the passing of the act, was no doubt also a contributory factor to the failure to enforce it in practice. It is important, none the less, to realize the significance of the fact that it was in the statute book, for by article XVIII of the Treaty of Union the laws in use within the Kingdom of Scotland were to remain in force as before, and, though alterable by the Parliament of Great Britain, were to remain unaltered 'except for evident utility of the subjects within Scotland'. In this way, the Scots undoubtedly secured a considerable advance in educational legislation over their English neighbours.

The Treaty of Union itself had no specific educational reference, but the Act of Security guaranteeing presbyterian church government, passed in the same year and regarded as virtually part and parcel of it, stipulated that 'the universities and colleges of St. Andrews, Glasgow, Aberdeen, and Edinburgh as now established by law shall continue within this Kingdom for ever'. The same statute also re-enacted certain provisions of an act of William and Mary of 1690, whereby in all time coming no professors, principals, regents, masters or others bearing office in any university, college or school within the kingdom should be admitted or allowed to continue in the exercise of their functions without acknowledging, professing and subscribing to the Confession of Faith, and themselves practising and conforming to the worship presently in use in the Church of Scotland. This requirement certainly gave the Established Church a considerable power over the educational system of the country, a power which, though generally not abused, led to friction in times when the danger of episcopacy had entirely passed away and been superseded by religious difficulties of a different character. On the whole, however, the national Church, finally entrenched at the Revolution of 1688, showed itself genuinely sympathetic to the furtherance of education and was largely responsible for what real progress was made in the establishment of parochial schools during the eighteenth century.

By 1709 the special problems caused by the Gaelic-speaking highlands and islands were already prompting many to press for a society associated with the Church in Scotland in a similar way to that in which the Society for Promoting Christian Knowledge, founded in 1698, was associated with the Church of England. To this end, Queen Anne by letters patent dated 25th May 1709 granted a charter incorporating the Society in Scotland for Propagating Christian Knowledge, for the purpose of raising voluntary contributions towards the increase of piety and virtue within Scotland, especially in the highlands, islands and remote corners, where error, idolatry, superstition and ignorance were alleged most to abound on account of the largeness of parishes and the scarcity of schools. Any teachers employed in the work of the society had to be examined and approved by the presbytery within whose bounds they normally resided, and the progress of the society was to be reported to the General Assembly of the Church from time to time. Within twenty years over eighty schools are said to have been provided, and the work of the society demanded increased powers. Accordingly, on 5th June 1738, George II issued a supplementary charter permitting vocational education in husbandry and housewifery, in trades and manufactures, or in manual occupations, to be provided in addition to the reading, writing and arithmetic originally sanctioned by way of instruction, and further empowering the society to sell and dispose of land and property as often as might be judged expedient and in the society's own interests.

The clamant need for the activities of the S.S.P.C.K. in the early part of the century in those districts where the Reformation had not penetrated is graphically stated by Graham. In the highlands during the seventeenth century, despite all efforts, schools had been unknown except in Argyllshire, and even where they existed, though reading, writing and the elements of religion were taught, all instruction was given in an unknown tongue. The result was that children who did not understand English were instructed by teachers who did not know Gaelic. In short, he asserts, there may be said to have been no education at all. Even the well-intentioned efforts of the Society, though a great improvement on what had gone before, were directed towards instructing the children in the principles of Christianity rather than towards elevating their intellectual and secular interests. As late as 1758 there were still 175 highland parishes without a school or schoolmaster. Not, indeed, that conditions even in the more progressive lowlands were by any means satisfactory by the most lenient standards. In 1715, in the county of Fife, only one in three of the male and one in twelve of the female population could sign their names. Five years later, in the more backward parts of the country such as Galloway, scarcely any of the common people were able to read, and even by the 1730's, though over 100 parish schools had been established in the barbarous highlands, there remained twelve parishes in the Presbytery of Ayr as yet unprovided with a school.

On the other hand, the teaching of the Church was much more effective and widespread in lowland districts and the incidence of private and unofficial schools much greater. Thus the inhabitants, though often illiterate, were not entirely ignorant and possessed in many cases a good deal of theological and Biblical information, albeit narrow and dogmatic in character. Nor were the heritors always to blame for the lack of a schoolmaster, for in many cases schools actually established in accordance with the statutory requirements remained for long periods vacant for lack of a qualified candidate to fill the post. The plain fact is that the stipulated salary, being originally based on the values of 1646 (fifty years earlier than the date at which it was made statutory), became, even where punctually paid, rapidly quite inadequate to maintain a teacher and his family in anything approaching comfort, and in addition the act had made no provision for a dwelling-house. This omission was, it is true, rectified by the first amending act, passed in 1803, which not only raised the statutory salary but laid upon the heritors the duty of providing a house for the schoolmaster, limited, however, to two apartments, and ground for a garden of not less than ¼ acre Scots. Nevertheless, it remains true that throughout the eighteenth century the teacher's was an unenviable lot.

Besides his basic salary, he had, of course, also his fees, but these rarely exceeded 1/- per quarter from each child for instruction in the 3 R's, or 2/- where Latin and the 'higher branches' were taught. The teacher was thus frequently compelled to supplement his income by undertaking other offices, such as those of precentor or session-clerk, or registrar of births, marriages and deaths. But in spite of these adverse conditions the parish schools of Scotland had a remarkable effect in promoting knowledge and instruction among the people. They were frequented by all classes from the highest to the lowest and offered instruction equally to the son of the laird and the child of the hind. Humble though they were, they generally succeeded in attracting the services of men of learning and scholarship, however lacking in pedagogic skill as judged by modern requirements. Since the master's main efforts were directed to the 'lad o' pairts', this defect passed unnoticed for the most part, and his other qualities opened to the more promising pupils professional posts in which many attained great distinction.

The distinguishing feature of the parish school was that it professed to be at once an elementary and a secondary school. In this way the best of them effected a wide diffusion of education to every class in the country, while also serving as a stepping-stone to the highest teaching of the universities. Though the latter were closed to women, the schools of the people were by no means confined to boys, and what is now termed 'co-education' has been the rule in the majority of Scottish educational institutions from the days of the Reformers. In the towns an intermediate link, representing the present-day 'secondary education', existed in the shape of burgh schools, many of which were likewise co-educational, but they also were mixed as regards the instruction provided. While generally of a higher academic standing than the parochial schools and offering a better preparation for university work, they had often to combine this function with instilling the rudiments of education into the heads of mere beginners. In the main, however, since their real concern was to provide instruction in Latin grammar, they normally required their pupils to have had a preliminary education in the vernacular to enable them at least to read and write, and such preliminary instruction was sometimes given in separate so-called 'English schools' up to the age of nine.

The parochial system did not extend to the burghs, but despite the absence of legislative enactments there had been 'grammar' (or burgh) schools in all the towns of any consequence in Scotland since before the Reformation. Unlike the parish schools, they were under local control, though the Church also claimed a certain measure of superintendence over them in the matter of approving appointments of staff. Nor was there any definite system of maintenance: generally a small stipend was paid out of the 'common good' of the burgh (i.e. public monies held in trust by the municipality) but where this failed a specific assessment for the upkeep of the school was not unknown. For the rest the master or masters depended upon the pupils' fees, but, notwithstanding occasional complaints to the contrary, the lot of the burgh schoolmaster was not an unhappy one, at least when compared with that of the parochial schoolmaster.

At the beginning of the century the curriculum was predominantly classical and chiefly Latin at that, for little Greek was taught. The explanation of this is to be found in the fact that, in default of a true vernacular of his own and through reluctance to accept English with its bitter associations, the Scot of the seventeenth century had clung to Latin as the most natural medium for literary expression longer than most other Europeans. Greek on the other hand tended to be regarded, except in its most elementary stages, as the prerogative of the university. So far was this carried, indeed, that for long no official instruction in Latin was provided by the universities, although Latin itself was the medium of instruction for the teaching given there. In consequence, a fairly thorough grounding was expected from the schools, but gradually the universities themselves appointed 'regents' of humanity (by which dignified title the study of Latin is still known in the Scottish universities), whose teaching, however, did not at first constitute an integral part of the curriculum, being largely preparatory to the real work of the university. Later its claims for inclusion among the subjects of higher teaching were recognized and both speaking of Latin and lecturing in that medium were discontinued in the course of the eighteenth century. The practice of teaching in English was initiated at Glasgow by the redoubtable Francis Hutcheson on his appointment to the chair of moral philosophy there in 1729.

But although Latin was practically the only subject taught in the larger grammar schools—and taught generally by means of a grammar written in Latin until the appearance of Thomas Ruddiman's famous *Rudiments* in 1714—some of the smaller burgh schools which by their remoteness escaped the cramping influence of the university offered a wider curriculum, including French, arithmetic, mathematics, navigation and drawing. Where more than one master was employed in a burgh school the system of rotation, characteristic of the universities also, was generally in force, whereby the masters or 'doctors' advanced in turn with their classes and on reaching the top of the school handed them over to the principal or 'rector'.

The change in attitude towards the place of Latin coincided with a period of greatly increased commercial prosperity towards the middle of the century, and as a natural consequence a demand arose for a more modern type of education beyond the elementary stage. This move is noticeable even in the modest activities of the S.S.P.C.K., which for lack of funds had been so far unable to take advantage of the powers conferred under its second charter. The opening up of the highlands after the Jacobite rebellion of 1745 seemed to offer a new opportunity, and in 1755 an organized effort was made by the Society to establish the rudiments of a system of technical education by the founding of spinning schools. At the same time a more liberal policy with regard to the language question was pursued in their ordinary schools, and after 1766 their schoolmasters, previously prohibited from teaching Gaelic, were instructed to teach their pupils to read both Gaelic and English in those parts of the highlands where Erse [*sic*] was the language generally spoken. By 1774, however, only twelve spinning schools had been established, six in Argyllshire, two in Inverness-shire, one in Elgin and one in Dunbartonshire. Nevertheless, progress was maintained and by 1783 the number was stated to exceed twenty, while in 1796 there were 94 such schools, estimated to be educating some 2,350 young people, chiefly girls. With the infiltration of the Industrial Revolution into Scotland there came a gradual decline and a tendency to convert the spinning into sewing schools, but there were still 89 of them in 1825 and 76 sewing schools in 1872. In the burghs the new movement towards a more practical education took the form of Writing or Commercial Schools, in which book-keeping, arithmetic and sometimes mathematics were taught. Schools of this type were established in Dumfries in 1723, in Stirling in 1747, and in Banff in 1762. In other places the reaction to the exclusively classical curriculum expressed itself in a reorganization of the course of study in the grammar school itself, as at Ayr, where the town council in 1746 greatly broadened the scheme of education given by adding a scientific element, consisting of mathematics, navigation, surveying, natural philosophy and book-keeping, to the existing curriculum of Latin and Greek.

But by far the most powerful influence was the complete revulsion from the classical curriculum which took place at Perth in 1760, where a petition to the town council put a cogent case for the advantages of science as against the grammatical knowledge of dead languages and skill in metaphysical subtleties which had hitherto constituted the whole of higher education in Scotland. As a result of this memorial the town council resolved to establish an entirely new type of school, to which the name 'academy' was given, and it was opened in due course in 1761. Not only were all teaching and exercises to be in English, but no provision at all was made for instruction in languages, and the scheme of study was confined entirely to modern subjects such as mathematics, natural science, astronomy, physics, English, civil history, the principles of religion and later chemistry, drawing and painting. This remarkable precedent rapidly stimulated emulation elsewhere, and similar academies were established in Dundee in 1786, Inverness in 1788, Elgin and Fortrose in 1791, Ayr in 1794 and Dumfries in 1802. Generally they were founded by public subscription and not, as in the case of the prototype at Perth, by the town council with the aid of public subscriptions. In consequence they normally had a separate body of management, on which the town council sometimes had representation. The curricula of these schools were not absolutely uniform, including occasionally additional subjects such as geography and French, but their influence undoubtedly introduced a much needed leaven into Scottish education.

Finally, university education made considerable headway in the course of the century. It had, to some extent, been reformed and unified by an act of the Scottish parliament of 1690 for Visitation of Universities, Colleges and Schools, which set up a parliamentary commission 'to take trial' of the present professors, principals, regents, masters and others bearing office. Its jurisdiction covered all the educational institutions of the country and it remained in session until 1700, but it was chiefly concerned with the universities, which it systematically purged from all taint of episcopalian influence. Despite the relative poverty of the country, there were no fewer than five university institutions in Scotland. The oldest, the University of St. Andrews, founded in 1411, had the collegiate constitution of the ancient English universities, though on a smaller scale, and had gradually acquired three colleges in the course of time: St. Salvator's in 1450, St. Leonard's in 1512 and St. Mary's in 1537. Originally they had all been colleges of arts and theology, but by the partial adoption of the Reformers' plan for specialization contained in the Nova Fundatio of 1579 St. Mary's College had since that date been exclusively theological. The University of Glasgow, founded in 1451, had never comprised more than one college, but subsequently somewhat futile endeavours were made from time to time to distinguish between the 'college' and the 'university' of Glasgow. The third university was established in Aberdeen in 1494 with the implicit design of civilizing the north of Scotland, and there too only one college, begun in 1500 and completed in 1505, was ever founded, originally known as the College of St. Mary-in-Nativitate but later called King's College in honour of James V. All three universities were medieval in origin, having been sanctioned by papal bull and royal charter, but owing their existence to the initiative of their respective local bishops, Wardlaw, Turnbull and Elphinstone.

Edinburgh, not being the seat of a bishopric, had had to wait until the Reformation before acquiring a seat of learning of its own, although there is evidence of an interest on the part of Robert Reid, the last Catholic bishop of Orkney, who died in 1558, in a project of founding a college there. No definite action was taken, however, until 1582, when King James VI granted a charter to the Town Council of Edinburgh authorizing the establishment of a college for the furtherance of education and learning in the city. It was opened in the following year and conferred its first degrees on 48 students in 1587, a privilege later confirmed by an act of the

Scottish parliament in 1621, but in contradistinction to its sister institutions the University of Edinburgh was essentially municipal in origin and throughout its history it suffered certain handicaps from its subjection to the authority of the municipality.

Lastly, in 1593, the fifth Earl Marischal founded a second college in Aberdeen bearing his own name; it was intended to constitute an entirely separate institution from the earlier medieval foundation. A royal charter, granted for this purpose by James VI in April 1593, was ratified by an act of the Scottish parliament in August of the same year but conditionally upon the college being subject to the jurisdiction of the Town Council of Aberdeen. Nevertheless, none of the difficulties which subsequently arose at Edinburgh seem to have beset Marischal College. The absurdity of having two autonomous universities within a mile of each other, each largely duplicating the work of the other, soon became apparent and endless efforts were made to bring the separate colleges at least under the same authority. This was nearly effected in 1641 when Charles I issued a charter of union incorporating the two institutions in a 'Universitas Carolina'. The union was even confirmed by an act of the Scottish parliament in the same year, but it seems to have been purely nominal, since each college retained its separate administration and when the act of ratification came within the rescissory act of 1661 the opportunity of drifting apart again was quickly seized by the college authorities. Thereafter they remained quite independent of one another, under the grandiose titles respectively of the 'university and King's College' and the 'Marischal College and university', until 1860.

At the beginning of the eighteenth century, though they were by no means uniform, the Scottish universities tended on the whole to conform to a common pattern. They virtually awarded only the degree of M.A., after a four years' course of study, although they also prepared candidates in theology for ordination to the Church of Scotland and in some cases provided rudimentary instruction in Medicine which later led up to the degree of M.D. But honorary doctorates in Divinity and likewise in Law, which was not yet taught in any of them, began also to be conferred. There can be little doubt, however, that the Arts course constituted the staple curriculum in all four universities at this time. It was still largely medieval in content and consisted chiefly of philosophy with a slight admixture of linguistic training and grammar. In general, Greek was taught in the first or bajan class, logic and metaphysics in the semi or second class, ethics and 'pneumatics' (covering such abstruse questions as the nature of angels, the human soul, and the one true God) in the tertian or bachelor class, and finally natural philosophy (including probably some mathematics) in the magistrand or fourth class.

The teaching was carried on by 'regents', who rotated with their class throughout the course and were therefore responsible for providing the whole encyclopaedic scheme of education, whatever their own personal bent might be. This lack of specialization, coupled no doubt with the relative over-supply of university institutions in proportion to the population of the country, distinctly militated against high standards of teaching, and already in the seventeenth century there had been a partial reaction against the regenting system in favour of specialist professors. This was particularly noticeable in the case of linguistic and mathematical studies and by the end of the century it had led to the establishment in Arts of separate chairs of Latin, Greek and mathematics, and in Divinity of a chair of Hebrew. Otherwise the system proved resistant to change and lingered on in some of the universities for a considerable part of the following century. It was first abolished at Edinburgh through the influence of the great

William Carstares in 1708, at Glasgow as a result of an act for better regulation of the university in 1727, at St. Andrews on the union of the colleges in 1747, but at Aberdeen not until 1753 in the case of Marischal College and 1799 in that of King's.

The Union of the Parliaments in 1707 had been followed by a period of relative stagnation in the life of the country in general, while the final abolition of episcopacy bore heavily on St. Andrews, the former ecclesiastical centre, in particular. Stripped of her importance she was even less able than her sister city of Aberdeen to support, though within the framework of a single university, two competing colleges engaged in duplicating each other's work, and was consequently obliged to pursue a policy of retrenchment by uniting the two Arts colleges of St. Salvator's and St. Leonard's, which was effected by act of parliament in 1747. Not even the abolition of regenting, though undoubtedly a progressive step, served immediately to raise the standard of learning in the country. On the contrary, by severing the tutorial relationship previously existing between master and student, one of its first effects was to lead to irregularity of studies and to discourage college residence. As a result, not only did the desirable custom of living in college gradually die out, but the practice of graduation in Arts, since students now tended to select only such classes as immediately met their requirements, dwindled practically to vanishing point in all the universities except the two Aberdeen colleges, in which the regenting system had been longest retained.

No doubt there was something to be said for regarding attendance at a university simply as part of an ordinary education, but the absence of any standard of entrance and the temptation for a professor to increase the meagre endowment of his chair by additional fees were bound to have unfavourable repercussions on the quality of the work done there, despite the fact that many of the occupants of chairs enjoyed European reputations as scholars. Indeed, there was no clear line of demarcation between school and university, and as a general rule students matriculated at far too early an age. This encroachment of the university into the proper sphere of the secondary school was perhaps inevitable in the circumstances of the time, but it seriously interfered with the harmonious development of an adequate system of intermediate education in the country and proved exceedingly difficult to eradicate.

So far as professional training was concerned, things were somewhat better, and as the century wore on considerable progress was made. Despite the union with England, Scotland had retained her own ecclesiastical and legal systems, and the universities found themselves called upon to provide a supply of theologians and jurists to manage affairs of Church and State. Theological training of a kind had, of course, always been given, but the standard was far from satisfactory, and throughout the eighteenth century it remained comparatively pedestrian. Nevertheless, there were signs of improvement quite early in the century; mention of Hebrew studies has already been made, and by 1716 there were regius chairs of ecclesiastical history at St. Andrews, Glasgow and Edinburgh. In the first twenty years of the century Edinburgh also laid the foundations of a flourishing law school by acquiring three chairs in Law and a chair of civil (or constitutional) history. Glasgow likewise built up something of a reputation for the teaching of law by the second half of the century.

But undoubtedly the most brilliant departure was in the field of Medicine, in which Scotland had always shown a pioneering spirit. As early as 1505 an Incorporation of Surgeons and Barbers, the first surgical fraternity in Great Britain, had been set up in Edinburgh, and this example was soon followed by the establishment of a Faculty of Physicians and Surgeons in Glasgow. Then in 1681 Charles II granted a charter authorizing a Royal College of

Physicians in Edinburgh and in 1694 the older incorporation was reconstituted as the Royal College of Surgeons. It cannot be claimed that an adequate course of medical instruction was provided by either of these agencies, but the very existence of extra-mural teaching stimulated competition in the university and medical degrees were conferred by it from 1705 onwards. In 1726 a regular Faculty of Medicine was instituted, and clinical instruction was made available by the establishment of a Royal Infirmary in 1746. By the end of the century the fame of the Edinburgh medical school had become world-wide and of the 150 annual graduates in medicine not more than one-third were native Scots. In Glasgow, too, shortly after the middle of the century there was systematic, if incomplete, medical training, but at Aberdeen and St. Andrews, though chairs of medicine existed, no organized teaching was given.

In spite of this, however, these two universities took advantage of the growing demand for Scottish medical qualifications to confer doctorates in Medicine quite indiscriminately on any candidates who were willing to pay the necessary fees. The inevitable result was to bring discredit upon Scottish degrees, and it was long before even the high reputation of Edinburgh and Glasgow could live down the contempt in which they were held. Nevertheless, interest in the related field of Science was aroused and in 1783 the Royal Society of Edinburgh was founded to encourage scientific inquiry and investigation. In the absence of any specific degree in Science many indeed appear to have taken the medical course without a definite intention of practising medicine. Thus, for instance, in the early part of the following century such famous figures as George Birkbeck, the pioneer of technical education in Great Britain, Sir James Kay-Shuttleworth, the founder of the English educational system, and not least Charles Darwin himself, had, though Englishmen, all been medical students at Edinburgh University.

PART II

THE FIRST HALF OF THE NINETEENTH CENTURY

CHAPTER II

ELEMENTARY EDUCATION TO 1864

THE impact of the Industrial Revolution was felt less acutely in Scotland than in England, where the beginning of the nineteenth century witnessed great activity in the sphere of primary education. Even so, however, there was evidence that the statutory parochial system was beginning to break down, and the increased prosperity of the latter part of the eighteenth century had, in particular, lowered the value of money to such an extent that the fixed salary of the schoolmaster had become insufficient. Since there was no machinery for revising the limits laid down in the Scotch act of 1696, an amending act was required. This was passed in 1803 and was known as the Parochial Schoolmasters (Scotland) Act.

By virtue of this measure the statutory minimum salary of the schoolmaster was raised from 100 to 300 merks (£16 3/4) per annum, and the maximum to 400 merks (£22 4/5). The manner of stating this increase was somewhat curious, since the coinage of Scotland had in the meantime been assimilated to that of England under the Treaty of Union in 1707. Provision was also made for revision of salaries every twenty-five years where necessary, and the value of a 'chalder' (about 96 bushels) of oatmeal was to be used as the criterion. Under section 8 of the act the heritors were required to provide a schoolhouse in every parish which was not already supplied with one, and in section 11 they were permitted to divide parishes of great extent or dense population among two or more teachers. This was an important extension to the existing educational resources of the country and resulted in the establishment of a new class of schools, known as 'side schools'. They resembled the older parochial schools in all respects, but in parishes where they were set up the heritors were excused the necessity of providing additional schoolhouses, and the total salary for which they might be assessed was not to exceed 600 merks per annum. In many parishes, however, the heritors went beyond the minimum requirements of the law.

The act laid down that schoolmasters were to be appointed by the minister and heritors who owned land within the parish of not less than £100 Scots (£8 6/8 sterling) of valued rent, and that the fees should be fixed by the same body. But all appointments were subject to the approval of the presbytery and the schoolmasters were required to sign the Confession of Faith and the formula of the Church of Scotland. The power of suspension and dismissal was also vested in the presbytery but the grounds on which action could be taken were limited to neglect of duty, immoral conduct or cruelty to the scholars. The minister of the parish was to superintend the work of the school but the hours of teaching and the length of the vacations were to be regulated by the presbytery. Thus the act perpetuated the close connection between the Church of Scotland and the statutory system of education that had already existed for over a century.

So far as it extended, the parochial system was reasonably successful, but it did not affect the larger towns at all and fell short in the country parishes of the highlands and islands in particular. With an area almost four-sevenths that of England and Wales, Scotland had only about one-fifteenth the number of parishes. The plight of the growing towns was, however, the more serious problem, and before long the Church took action to supply the lack of elementary schools in urban districts. This action was not corporate but depended on the initiative of the kirk session of local congregations. Many of these founded and managed what came to be known as 'sessional schools', of which perhaps the most famous was the one founded in connection with the Tron Church in Edinburgh by John Wood in 1813. In time these schools numbered over a hundred and catered for nearly 12,000 pupils but they were altogether inadequate to meet the needs of the large centres of population.

As Scotland was still a predominantly agricultural country, official action was first taken to increase the number of parishes in the remoter districts. This was effected in 1824 by an act of parliament authorizing the building of additional places of worship in the highlands and islands of Scotland. The new parishes thus created were, however, for ecclesiastical purposes only and were known as *quoad sacra*. Attention having been focussed on these districts, the Church of Scotland decided in the same year to set up a permanent Education Committee with powers to increase the means of education, particularly in the highlands and islands. This committee was responsible for the erection and maintenance of some 200 schools, which were financed by the General Assembly of the Church and came to be called, in consequence, 'assembly schools'. So far as possible the instruction given in these schools was similar to that provided in the parish schools, and in token of its desire to keep them undenominational, the Church threw them open to the children of Roman Catholic parents in 1829.

In the meantime, the parish system of Scotland, inadequate though it was, was frequently made the basis of attempted legislation for the establishment of a similar system in England. In 1807, for instance, Samuel Whitbread had included in his Poor Law Reform Bill a scheme for establishing parochial schools. Then, in 1820, Henry Brougham, who had been educated in Edinburgh and was a great admirer of the Scottish system, introduced a Parish Schools Bill into the House of Commons. Finally, in 1833, John Arthur Roebuck made the most ambitious attempt of all by proposing 'universal and national education of the whole people' under a ministry of public instruction working through local committees with powers of compulsion on all children between 6 and 12 years of age. Had this bill been passed it would have advanced the cause of education by forty years, but it was defeated largely on the grounds of cost. Nevertheless, it was not entirely without its effects on the course of educational developments. In the following month, as a kind of solatium, Parliament voted a grant of £20,000 for the erection of schoolhouses for the education of the poorer classes in Great Britain. By a Treasury minute of August 1833 this sum was made to last until 31st March 1834, but thereafter it was annually renewed by Parliament until 1839. At first no special machinery was set up to supervise the disbursement of this money but the commissioners of the Treasury required the sponsorship in England of either of the two voluntary bodies, the National Society or the British and Foreign School Society.

The need for schoolhouses being presumably less acute in Scotland, no part of the first grant was allocated to that part of Great Britain. In 1834, 1836, 1837 and 1838, however, separate grants of £10,000 in each of these years were assigned to Scotland, and in 1838 an act was also passed to extend the parochial system of schools to the *quoad sacra* parishes created fourteen years earlier. The new schools were popularly known as 'parliamentary schools', and, as before, the heritors were obliged to provide the building and a house for the schoolmaster, but on this occasion the Treasury undertook to find the annual salary. Accordingly, the sum of £6,000 from the grant of 1837 and a further sum of £4,000 from the grant of 1838 were set aside for this purpose. In 1839, however, the system of separate grants was discontinued and in that year a consolidated grant of £30,000 was voted for public education in Great Britain. At the same time, it was felt desirable to institute some kind of check upon the application of the sums voted by Parliament for the purpose of promoting public education. As a result, a committee of the Privy Council on education, consisting of the Lord President, the Lord Privy Seal, the Home Secretary and the Chancellor of the Exchequer, was constituted by order in council. It was the first body to have control over public expenditure on education, and by supreme good fortune Dr. James Kay, a medical graduate of Edinburgh University and an enlightened educationist, was appointed permanent Secretary to the new committee.

Under the aegis of Kay (or Kay-Shuttleworth, as he came later to be called) the scope of the grants was gradually extended to cover maintenance and teachers' salaries as well as school buildings. In June 1839 the Committee of Council announced that in future grants would carry the right of inspection with them and steps were taken to appoint the first H.M. Inspectors of schools. This decision caused something of a stir in England, where educational provision was almost entirely on a voluntary basis, with the result that in the first instance inspection was put upon a denominational basis also. Accordingly, in 1840, a concordat was reached with the Church of England, the nonconformists and the Church of Scotland, whereby the Rev. John Allen, Mr. S. Tremenheere and Mr. J. Gibson were respectively appointed inspectors of the schools under the management of these bodies. In the same year the Committee began to issue directives in the form of minutes, which were collected in annual volumes until 1860, when they were for the first time digested into a 'code'. At the same time the annual grant for education steadily increased and by 1848 had risen to £125,000. The Scottish schools, however, did not require to avail themselves of grants, unless they chose to submit to the conditions of the Committee of Council in order to increase their statutory revenue derived from the heritors, and the great majority did not in fact take advantage of them.

In 1843 the Disruption of the Church of Scotland caused an unexpected extension of educational facilities throughout the country. This event was the outcome of an unfortunate act passed in 1712, during the reign of Queen Anne, restoring patronage to livings in the Church of Scotland. The measure was regarded in Scotland as a violation of the spirit of the Treaty of Union, but despite repeated attempts to have it repealed during the eighteenth century it remained in force. It culminated in a secession of 470 ministers of the Church of Scotland under the leadership of Dr. Thomas Chalmers in 1843 and resulted in the formation of the Free Church of Scotland. As about 80 parochial schoolmasters—who by the act of 1803 were required to sign the formula of the Church of Scotland—and some 280 teachers in assembly, S.S.P.C.K. and other schools connected with the Church of Scotland joined the new denomination, it became necessary to make provision for them. In consequence, the Free Church decided to set up a system of schools similar to that of its sister Church, chiefly as a means of absorbing these displaced schoolmasters, and within the next five years it had founded over 500 elementary schools to supplement the work of those already in existence. As the only H.M. Inspector of schools had also joined the Free Church, the inspectorate was enlarged by the appointment of another inspector of Established Church schools in the person of Mr. John Gordon, who had been the first Secretary to the Education Committee of the Church of Scotland. Thus, however disturbing to the ecclesiastical unity of the country, the Disruption brought considerable educational expansion.

In the meantime, a certain amount of educational experiment outside the official system was being carried on by social reformers. It was particularly notable in the sphere of infant education and is mainly associated with the names of Robert Owen and David Stow. Owen was an industrialist of Welsh origin who in the early years of the century endeavoured in his mills at New Lanark to show that the new industrial system could be utilized to improve the conditions of the working class in sanitation, welfare, leisure and education. He expanded his views in his treatise *A New View of Society* in 1813, but also gave practical expression to them by fixing the minimum age for employment at 10 years and providing free schools for the children of his employees who were between 5 and 10 years old. In 1816 he opened a nursery school for children as young as 18 months. He adapted the instruction to suit the pupils' requirements by confining the teaching mainly to conversation and the showing of pictures and by providing social activities such as dancing, singing and games. One of his infant teachers, James Buchanan, was later sent to take charge of a similar school set up at Westminster by the enthusiastic band of reformers known as the 'education-mad' party, which included in its membership James Mill and Joseph Hume, both of them Scotsmen, in addition to the indefatigable Henry Brougham. Under their auspices another infant school was set up at Spitalfields and placed in the charge of Samuel Wilderspin, who was instrumental in the founding of the London Infant School Society in 1824.

In Scotland the movement was continued by David Stow, a Glasgow philanthropist engaged in commerce. As early as 1811 he was dismayed by the amount of deceit and wickedness he saw around him and began to devote his leisure time to mission work in the poorer parts of the city. In 1816 he began a Sunday School in an effort to check delinquency by catching children young, but experience showed that more persistent efforts were required to counteract the forces of daily routine. Stow therefore founded a day school, in which he wished to begin with children under six years of age, when their intellectual and moral habits would not be fully formed. As a result of his efforts the Glasgow Infant School Society was founded in 1826 and Stow began to turn his attention to the problem of training teachers to implement his educational ideals. This was at first accomplished by adding a training department to the existing school, through which a hundred teachers passed in the next ten years, but it was soon apparent that a separate training college, or 'normal school', was required. In 1834 the Society was reconstituted, as the Glasgow Educational Society, to take over the financial burden of Stow's model schools, for infants in the Drygate and for older children in the Saltmarket, and to evolve out of them a normal seminary 'for the training of teachers in the most approved modes of intellectual and moral training'. Like Owen, Stow combined theory with practice and propounded what he called a 'training system', as applied to the education of young children, which was based on his observations and experience. It included nearly all the best features of modern educational practice, and was greatly in advance of its time.

The increasing pressure of work at the Committee of Council's office, which was quite inadequately staffed, brought about the resignation of Kay-Shuttleworth on grounds of ill-health at the early age of 45, in December 1849. It soon became apparent that the highly centralized system that had evolved since 1833 necessitated some form of reorganization. Hitherto only elementary education had been subsidized, but the International Exhibition of 1851 revealed a deficiency of technical education and steps were taken to remedy this defect. As early as 1836 the Committee of Council on Trade (forerunner of the Board of Trade) had been given a Treasury grant to set up what was termed a Normal School of Design, with a view to teaching the principles of art as applied to industry and commerce.

As a result of the experiences of 1851 it was developed into a Department of Practical Art in 1852; a Department of Science was added in 1853. The combined 'Science and Art Department' came to be housed at South Kensington, and its function was to establish special science schools in selected localities and to distribute grants to state-aided elementary schools which complied with its regulations for the teaching of science in addition to the other recognized subjects.

A source of unfavourable comparison with European countries was the publication in 1846 of parts of Horace Mann's Seventh Report to the Massachusetts Board of Education under the title of *Report of an Educational Tour*. The document was edited by Dr. W. B. Hodgson, a well-known Scottish educationist, and contained a highly entertaining account of Mann's visit to Europe in 1843. The pages dealing with Scottish schools, which he regarded as second only to those of Holland, are among the most amusing in pedagogic literature, though his editor considered that he had been too favourably impressed by what he had seen. On the English system—or the lack of it—he was, on the other hand, very severe, and his strictures no doubt stimulated a series of unsuccessful bills, designed to establish a better integrated educational system, which were introduced into parliament between 1850 and 1855. On the failure of these measures an order in council set up in February 1856 what amounted to a new branch of the Civil Service, called the 'Education Department'. It incorporated the former Committee of Council on Education and relieved the Committee of Council on Trade of responsibility for the Science and Art Department. The Lord President remained the official head, but since he was in those days almost invariably a peer, the order made provision for a Vice-President of the Committee of Council who should henceforth be the responsible minister in the House of Commons. Like its two constituent elements, the Education Department had jurisdiction in Scotland despite the differences in educational tradition.

These were not long in coming to a head. Sir John Pakington, sponsor of one of the ill-fated education bills, being still dissatisfied with the educational situation, proposed a Royal Commission of Inquiry. This was appointed under the chairmanship of the Duke of Newcastle in 1858. The commission's terms of reference were to inquire into the state of popular education in England, and to report what measures were required for the extension of sound and cheap elementary instruction to all classes of the people. The economic aspect was stressed partly on account of the heavy expenditure on the Crimean War of 1854-6 and partly on account of the ever increasing sums spent on education. In 1859, for instance, the annual grant was more than forty times what it had been in 1833.

Meanwhile in Scotland several law cases revealed the unsatisfactory situation which had resulted from the Disruption as regards the control of the Established Church over the appointment of schoolmasters, and an act dealing with the position was passed in 1861 under the title of the Parochial and Burgh Schoolmasters (Scotland) Act. This measure excused parochial schoolmasters from signing the Confession of Faith or formula of the Church of Scotland, and transferred the powers of examining them from the presbyteries to the universities, which for the purpose were grouped into regions. The University Court in each of the four districts was required to appoint six examiners, three professors in the Faculty of Arts and three in the Faculty of Divinity, who were to be remunerated by the Treasury. Under section 22 burgh schoolmasters were relieved entirely of presbyterial supervision, but parochial schoolmasters were obliged to sign an undertaking that they would teach nothing opposed to the Scriptures or the doctrine of the Shorter Catechism. The power of dismissing parochial schoolmasters for immorality or cruelty under the act of 1803 was now vested in the sheriff in place of the presbytery, but charges of negligence or incompetence were left in the hands of the minister and heritors, who were also permitted to grant a retiring allowance of two-thirds of the full salary. The act also raised the minimum salary to £35 and the maximum to £80 per annum, and authorized the employment of women teachers, at a maximum salary of £30 per annum, to give instruction in female industrial and household training as well as elementary education. Under section 5, therefore, what were known as 'heritors' girls' schools' were established, but the employment of women teachers in parochial schools had previously been connived at, since grants for training schoolmistresses had already been in operation in Scottish training colleges for twelve years. By this act the statutory control of the Established Church over the educational system of the country was largely superseded, and the way was paved for state action.

In the same year the report of the Newcastle Commission in England made its appearance, disclosing considerable inefficiency in the lower classes and general irregularity of attendance at inspected schools. Despite these defects of the existing system the commissioners were inclined to complacency, but suggested in their report that the only way of securing increased efficiency was to institute a searching individual examination of each pupil and to make the teacher's position dependent upon the results of it. This ill-advised recommendation, however innocently put forward, was the means of introducing into educational practice the disastrous principle of 'payment by results'. It was quickly seized upon by the Vice-President of the Committee of Council, Robert Lowe, who had in the previous year codified the Department's minutes and now lost no time in issuing a 'Revised Code'. This was presented to the House of Commons in July 1861 and was intended to apply to the disbursement of grants for 1862, although it was subsequently postponed until 1863.

The Department had, it is true, already introduced, in 1853, a capitation grant, based on attendance, to supplement the local income of rural schools, and extended it to borough schools in 1856. This grant was, however, confined to England and Wales, although in general no distinction was made between Scotland and England in the allocation of public money. By a minute of 9th May 1862 all grants were in future to be on a capitation basis and made dependent partly on attendance and partly on the proficiency of the individual pupil in the three elementary subjects of reading, writing and arithmetic at the discretion of H.M. Inspectors of Schools. Of a total grant of 12/- per child on the roll, 4/- was payable for attendance (fixed at two hundred attendances) and 2/8 for each of the three subjects of examination. Individual examination was not to apply to children under six, but for the others specified tests in reading, writing and arithmetic were laid down in six gradations of difficulty, known as standards. While it is true that the standard in which a child was to be examined was to be fixed by its capacity rather than its age, this provision was largely nullified by the fact that no child might be presented for examination a second time in the same or a lower standard, however bad its failure in a given standard might have been.

The revised code certainly introduced into elementary schools some notion of organization, where before—and especially in Scotland—there had largely been chaos. Indeed, the evidence goes to show that the charge of neglecting the lower forms in favour of the upper ones was even more applicable to the parish schools of Scotland than to the elementary schools of England, against which it had been made. In the Scottish schools the schoolmaster's attention was frequently almost entirely directed to the 'lad o' pairts' who was the pride of the school. At the same time, Scotsmen had been accustomed to regarding their parochial schools as something more than places confined merely to the rudiments of education, and they objected to receiving grants only in respect of the three R's. Another source of irritation was a new insistence on the fact that the government grant was intended to promote the education 'of children belonging to the classes who support themselves by manual labour'. Here again Scotsmen prided themselves that their public schools were not restricted to any particular class of pupils and resented the introduction of social distinctions in the allocation of public money for educational purposes. So-called 'elementary schools' in Scotland were thus 'mixed' in a double sense unknown in England: in the first place, they served as a link with the universities by providing advanced instruction, in addition to the elements; in the second place, they catered for children of all classes. It is hardly surprising, therefore, that the revised code began to make Scotland aware of the disadvantages of being tied to England under one central authority for education. Furthermore, the code had been imposed on Scotland largely as a result of an examination confined to English schools, which had consequently made no investigation of the situation in Scotland.

In view of widespread protests it was agreed in June 1864 to suspend the financial provisions of the Revised Code pending the appointment of a Royal Commission to inquire into the schools of Scotland. But the Department insisted on enforcing the principle of individual examination, even although the payment of the grant was not affected by the results of the annual inspection. Thus Scotland contrived to secure a breathing-space, which lasted for ten years, from the worst effects of the Revised Code, and continued to enjoy the old privileges of grants for maintaining training colleges, for building elementary schools, for augmenting the salaries of certificated teachers, for paying pupil teachers and for remunerating headmasters to whom the latter were attached. In the meantime, inspection by individual examination of pupils had the salutary effect of compelling many of the parochial schoolmasters to devote a greater amount of time to instructing the less able of their pupils in the elementary subjects.

CHAPTER III

HIGHER EDUCATION BEFORE 1860

(*a*) The Schools

The outstanding characteristic of Scottish secondary education at the beginning of the nineteenth century was a complete lack of direction. There was no uniformity or standard of aim. On the one hand, the ancient burgh or grammar schools in some towns, such as Glasgow, Stirling and Montrose, obstinately confined their teaching for long to the old classical curriculum of Latin and Greek, in the teeth of the modern reaction. On the other hand, the newly founded academies in other towns, such as Perth and Dundee, set up an equally strong current in favour of a wholly practical and utilitarian scheme of education. Occasionally, as in Edinburgh, it proved possible for the two types of school to co-exist, but generally, in default of a system of central control, a measure of compromise inevitably resulted. That is to say, while the study of classics was usually retained, provision was likewise made for the more practical subjects, or *vice versa*.

Thus, in many instances a move was made for amalgamation of the two types of school, and this often included also the former 'English' and newer 'Writing' schools, where these existed. In Perth and Dundee such incorporations were effected in 1807 and 1829 respectively, and elsewhere similar unions came about, in Kirkcudbright and Montrose, for example, in 1815. Where this happened, however, a confusion in nomenclature frequently resulted, since the combined institutions, though differing in an important respect from the wholly modern academies of the eighteenth century, tended to appropriate their title of 'academy'. Indeed, the ancient designation of 'grammar school', still characteristic of sister institutions in England, was retained only in relatively few cases, as in Aberdeen and Musselburgh, for where a burgh school was reformed under the newer influences without actual incorporation with an academy, the term 'high school' was often adopted to indicate the change, as in Edinburgh and Glasgow. In short, the academies generally succeeded in absorbing or even entirely superseding—as in Inverness and Ayr—the older grammar schools, and but rarely entered into a sustained rivalry with them.

The consequence of this educational activity, while certainly stimulating the demand for higher instruction and leading to increased enrolments and larger staffs, was also to take the management of many schools out of the control, usually sagacious, of public bodies like town councils and transfer it to the less experienced hands of boards of directors. The result was largely educational anarchy. No doubt other developments of the period were contributory to the general administrative confusion. In smaller burghs during the eighteenth century it had sometimes been customary, for instance, to unite with a neighbouring parish, on grounds of economy, to provide a mixed burgh and parochial school. Such an arrangement naturally necessitated adequate representation of the local heritors in the management of the combined school. The earliest example of this dates as far back as 1607 in Inveraray, but as late as 1821 a case occurred in Crail in Fifeshire.

The earlier half of the nineteenth century was conspicuous also for the foundation of a number of endowed schools in the hands of private trustees. In 1818, for instance, Dollar Institution (later renamed Academy) was set up out of funds left by John McNabb. In 1831 the

Madras College, St. Andrews, was endowed by the Rev. Dr. Andrew Bell, in commemoration of his so-called 'Madras system' of instruction, but on condition that it absorbed the previously existing grammar school. The Madras Academy in Cupar (also endowed by Dr. Bell and later reconstituted as the Bell-Baxter School), Milne's Institution in Fochabers, the Ewart Institution in Newton Stewart, the Bathgate Academy in West Lothian and Morrison's Academy in Crieff all owed their existence to private benefactors during this period. Finally, the current of reform active at the time in the great Public Schools of England, which culminated in the appointment of Thomas Arnold as headmaster of Rugby in 1828, seems also to have had some influence in fostering the growth of a small number of proprietary boarding schools in Scotland. The first of these was Loretto School, founded in 1829, though it did not achieve any great reputation until it was taken over in 1862 by the great Dr. H. H. Almond. It was closely followed by the opening of Merchiston Castle School in 1833. In 1841 a more ambitious project was launched by the Episcopal Church in Scotland, more explicitly on the lines of the English Public Schools with their strong Anglican tradition. It was the establishment of a school for some 150 or 200 pupils which would combine general education with domestic discipline and systematic religious superintendence; with the assistance of public subscriptions Trinity College, Glenalmond, was opened in 1847. The management was vested in six Scottish bishops, three other clergy and ten laymen.

It is not to be supposed that this absence of uniformity in external control was not reflected in the internal organization of these widely diverging types of school. In general, it had not been customary in Scotland to grant the headmaster (or 'rector', as he was traditionally called) any very extensive authority over his other colleagues on the staff. Though nominally in charge of the internal affairs of the school, he had only limited powers of discipline, hardly any control of appointments to the staff, and little to do with regulating the work done, since there was no compulsory course of studies and normally a separate fee was charged for each subject taken, at the option of the parent. This inherent anarchy was increased by the fusion of grammar schools and academies, when in some places two rectors were retained, as in Perth, and in others the office of rector was abolished altogether, as in Dundee. In either case there was a tendency for the virtually independent heads of the separate departments to form a council of masters, sometimes presided over by each in turn, to manage the internal affairs of the school in republican fashion. Even to this day, though notions have changed and a fully-fledged rector sits in authority over all, the head of each department of study at Dundee High School (so called since 1859) retains the title of headmaster (e.g. of mathematics, modern languages, etc.). Strangely enough, this competitive system seemed to commend itself to Scottish opinion as good for the school, and in some cases local sentiment was resolutely against consolidation of the work under one headmaster. As the century advanced, however, it became more usual to appoint a rector with a good deal of influence in all matters affecting the school, as in Inverness Royal Academy and in Glasgow in both High School and Academy. In a few cases, on the other hand, particularly where English influence made itself felt, as in the case of Edinburgh Academy, the headmaster was from the first granted supreme authority over the working of the whole school, with the power to appoint and dismiss his staff almost at pleasure. Thus the variations within the system were great.

Nor was there a greater measure of unanimity about what should constitute the proper content of the secondary curriculum. In the universities, it is true, there had been during the later eighteenth century a slight revival of classical scholarship, as distinct from the traditional devotion to the study of philosophy, and this movement received some support from the proposals of the University Commissioners of 1826-30 for the reform of the Arts curriculum. So far as the schools were concerned it led to a considerable improvement in the study of Greek in particular, which had been largely neglected during the eighteenth century except in a small number of schools, but it also served to restore the classics to favour generally. The study of mathematics received an impetus from the same source, for despite its importance in the study of natural philosophy it does not seem previously to have been regarded as an essential part of the Arts curriculum, save at Edinburgh from 1809. For the remainder of the nineteenth century, however, Latin, Greek and mathematics were securely established in all secondary and many parochial schools as 'the university subjects', where higher education was the objective.

On the modern side, on the other hand, a much greater degree of uncertainty existed, clearly showing the confusion of ideas regarding the relationship of the different subjects. For long arithmetic was taught with writing and not as part of mathematics; English and even modern languages were treated as a subordinate department of classics instead of being taught by separate masters; and science, so far from receiving specialist treatment, was in some cases lumped together with literature, history, and geography under the caption of 'general knowledge'. And until the practice of instituting an inclusive fee superseded the custom of charging separate fees for the various subjects, vested interests prevented such questions from being impartially thrashed out. At best, it was a period of experimentation which eventually proved instructive and was not without influence in widening the grammar school curriculum in England. As an example of the progressive spirit may be cited the celebrated James Pillans's introduction of the monitorial system of the English elementary school into the Edinburgh High School in 1810. It was the first application of the method to a secondary school in Great Britain, though it was imitated by Russell at Charterhouse in the following year, and it is not necessarily condemnatory to say that the experiment turned out to be a failure.

To increase the confusion, the Church also from time to time asserted its right of superintendence over burgh schools in virtue of a Scottish act of 1693 entitled 'Act for Settling the Quiet and Peace of the Church', by which all schoolmasters and teachers of youth in schools were declared to be liable to the trial, judgment and censure of the presbyteries of the bounds for their sufficiency, qualifications and deportment in their office. It mattered little that public opinion was out of sympathy with the assertion of obsolete rights of the kind, for the law courts were compelled to support them, and particularly after the Disruption of 1843 the position became ludicrous. Thus, at Campbeltown Grammar School the burgh schoolmaster was deposed by the local presbytery for joining the Free Church, and in 1850 similar legal action was taken, eventually with success, against two masters at Elgin Academy (formed in 1800 by amalgamation with the grammar and English schools of the burgh), on the grounds that it too was a public high school. Naturally, so scandalous an abuse of powers could not be allowed to continue and in 1861 the Parochial and Burgh Schoolmasters Act finally swept away all vestiges of ecclesiastical jurisdiction over statutory schools. But even by 1866 the Argyll Commissioners had found cause for considerable disagreement on vital questions of internal discipline and organization in secondary schools, such as whether or not there should be a rector with subordinate masters, or masters with coordinate powers; whether there should be a fixed curriculum, or parents should be left to select what subjects they deemed advisable; whether promotion from class to class should be regulated by routine or proficiency; whether each master should have his own class and pocket the fees, or the fees should be paid into a common fund. There was thus no strong line of demarcation between a general and a special education and no definite degree to which each was the responsibility of the secondary school when the Education Act of 1872 was passed. Consequently, there was no pretence of giving a real technical training of any sort either to adults or children.

Nevertheless, it is only fair to mention the pioneer work in the development of technical education which took place at the time of the Industrial Revolution. The lectures delivered at Anderson's Institution in Glasgow (later the Glasgow and West of Scotland Technical College) formed the beginning of technical education in Great Britain. Founded in 1796 under the will of John Anderson, Professor of Natural Philosophy at Glasgow University, the Institution had the good fortune to attract George Birkbeck as the second occupant of its chair of natural philosophy, from 1799 to 1804. In 1800 he established special courses of lectures for working mechanics, to help them to understand the principles of the type of work in which they were engaged, and after his departure Birkbeck's successor, Andrew Ure, carried on this innovation. In 1823, however, there was a split between the popular element and the rest of the Institution and the Glasgow Mechanics' Institution, the prototype of the mechanics' institutes which rapidly sprang up in England in the new industrial conditions, was founded, though subsequently reunited with the parent body. In 1821 a 'School of Arts' (later the Heriot-Watt College) was founded in Edinburgh for the better education of the mechanics of the city in such branches of physical science as were of practical application in their several trades, but it is an interesting commentary on this movement that sixty years later the Samuelson Commission on Technical Education concluded that the best possible preliminary to good technical instruction was a good secondary education.

(*b*) The Universities

During the eighteenth century the standard of teaching and learning had been progressively raised in most of the Scottish universities, particularly in the case of Edinburgh and Glasgow. Not only had specialist professors replaced the traditional regents but side by side with the old-established Divinity Halls new professional schools of Medicine and Law had grown up. In consequence of this it is hardly surprising that at the beginning of the nineteenth century the University of Edinburgh began to resent its anomalous position of dependence upon the municipality. Differences between the Senatus Academicus and the Town Council had occasionally arisen in the past but they became more acute about 1815, and by 1825 the deadlock was so serious that the Town Council threatened legal proceedings. The Senatus Academicus, on the other hand, appealed to the Home Secretary to set up a Royal Commission to settle the dispute, which turned on an academic matter, by arbitration. In August 1826 a commission of visitation was appointed by George IV, not to deal exclusively with the affairs of Edinburgh but to review and report upon all the universities and colleges of Scotland. By this time, indeed, the question of arbitration had been taken out of their hands, for the Town Council had already initiated legal proceedings to obtain a definition of their powers over the University in academic as well as administrative matters. In November 1827 the Court of Session decided that their jurisdiction in terms of the original foundation extended to matters of studies and that in consequence the Senatus had no right of making regulations in contradiction to those of the Town Council. On appeal this decision was upheld in January 1829, and that ended the litigation for the time being.

In the meantime the Royal Commission got down to business and continued to sit for a period of four years. As it was the first general inquiry into university education in Scotland since the parliamentary commission of 1690, the information it collected about the state of the Scottish universities at the beginning of the nineteenth century was extremely valuable. The commission originally consisted of 17 members, with the Earl of Aberdeen as chairman, but it was shortly afterwards increased to 22 members and presided over by the Earl of Rosebery, in whose favour the first chairman resigned. Under Lord Rosebery the commission carried on its labours until October 1830, when its report was finally completed. This massive volume comprised a general report on university education as well as particular reports on the individual universities, and it was ordered by the House of Commons to be published in October 1831.

Among the great variety of topics dealt with, the commissioners' recommendations as to the constitutions that should be adopted and the regulations for graduation which they proposed are the most interesting. Under the first head, the commissioners found that in each university, except Edinburgh, the principal and professors constituting the Senatus Academicus wielded almost unlimited authority in all academic and administrative matters. While agreeing that the original charters of the universities of St. Andrews, Glasgow and Aberdeen conferred certain powers upon the principals and professors of these institutions, the commissioners felt that they also implied 'some authority to which all members of the university might be subject'. On the other hand, they commented on the lack of a definite constitution in the case of Edinburgh and recognized that although in this instance there was some such authority, the actual system in force was 'very imperfectly adapted' to the requirements of a university. The commissioners accordingly proposed that the constitutions of all the Scottish universities be largely assimilated. As a first step they advocated the emancipation of the University of Edinburgh from the control of the Town Council (though the latter would retain its patronage of the University chairs) and the union of the two autonomous colleges in Aberdeen into a single university. In the universities other than Edinburgh it was already customary to elect a chancellor for life and a rector for a limited period, but at Edinburgh there were no such offices. There had never been a chancellor at any time since its foundation, and although the office of rector had been created for Alexander Henderson in 1640 it had been combined with that of Lord Provost by an act of the Town Council in 1665 and had virtually lapsed. The commissioners being assured that 'if attended with no other benefit', the institution of a chancellorship 'would eminently contribute to the respectability and dignity of the university', recommended that a chancellor, nominated for life by the Crown, should be forthwith appointed.

The commissioners also proposed to re-establish the office of rector on an entirely new basis. They proposed that the rector at Edinburgh should be elected for a period of seven years by the principal, professors and graduates of the University and that he should not be a principal or professor in any university. In the other universities his term of office was to be limited to four years and there were slight variations in the proposed mode of election, but otherwise the arrangements were to be similar. In all the universities the rector was to act as chairman of a new governing body, to be called the University Court, whose function it would be to supersede the administrative control exercised by the Town Council at Edinburgh and to supply the total lack of it in the remaining institutions.

The other members were to be the principal *ex officio*

and assessors appointed by chancellor and rector. At Edinburgh two additional assessors were to be nominated by the Town Council and by the principal, professors and graduates of the University. At St. Andrews the other principal was to be a member *ex officio*. At Glasgow the Dean of Faculties and the minister of Glasgow were to be members *ex officiis* and an assessor was to be elected by the principal, professors and graduates. Finally, in Aberdeen an additional assessor was to be nominated by the principal and professors only. Assessors generally, like the rector, were prohibited from being principals or professors in any university, but in one or two cases this was not stipulated (e.g. two assessors at Edinburgh and one at Aberdeen). To these University Courts extensive powers affecting the well-being of the university were to be delegated. They included the right of reviewing the regulations and decisions of the Senatus Academicus, originating and effecting improvements in the internal organization of the university, determining the duties of professors, fixing class fees, acting as a court of appeal from the Senatus, censuring or suspending professors after due investigation and exercising a general control over the revenue and expenditure of the university. Most of these duties had previously fallen to the Senatus Academicus, except at Edinburgh, and the latter was now to be restricted to maintaining the ordinary discipline of the university.

Under the head of graduation the commissioners found themselves confronted by an equally lax state of affairs. In Arts all the universities granted the degree of M.A. as a first degree, except Glasgow, which had somewhat unsucessfully revived the old B.A., but only in the two Aberdeen colleges was graduation in Arts taken at all seriously. In Divinity and Law the degrees of D.D. and LL.D. were purely honorary distinctions. Even in Medicine the degree of M.D. was, especially at St. Andrews, not always awarded with adequate safeguards. The commissioners therefore proposed to regulate graduation in all four faculties. In Arts they devised a four years' curriculum for the degree of B.A. It embraced double courses in Latin, Greek and mathematics, and single courses in logic and metaphysics, moral philosophy and natural philosophy. They recommended that in certain cases this degree might be awarded with honours of two classes, designated 'highest honours' and 'honourable distinction'. For the M.A. they prescribed a further year's study, entailing attendance at the classes of political economy, natural history and chemistry, and involving a specialized examination in literature, philosophy or science at the option of the candidate. In Divinity the commissioners proposed the institution of the degree of B.D., to be taken by graduates in Arts after a four years' course in theology, Hebrew, ecclesiastical history and Biblical criticism. They recommended that in future the D.D. degree should be conferred only on B.D.s of not less than five years' standing. In Law, on the other hand, no new degree was proposed, but the existing degree of LL.D. was to be made subject to examination following upon a three years' course in civil law, Scots law and conveyancing. The commissioners remarked, however, that a full course of instruction was available only in the University of Edinburgh. As in Divinity, the Law degree was to be made conditional on prior graduation in Arts.

Finally, in Medicine the existing M.D. was also to be retained but awarded only after the successful completion of a regular four years' course. It should not be conferred on candidates under the age of 21, and the commissioners thought that a thesis in addition to examination should no longer be required. In this instance they did not insist on graduation in Arts as a necessary preliminary but recommended that all candidates not so qualified should be required to pass a satisfactory examination to be conducted by the Faculty of Arts in Latin, Greek, mathematics and natural philosophy. In all the faculties the commissioners considered that the existing practice of professors acting as sole examiners to their own students was undesirable, but only for graduation in Arts did they make specific recommendations regarding the appointment of additional examiners. In Medicine, however, they expressed approval of the growing practice of conducting examinations in English instead of Latin.

In individual universities the commissioners freely recommended the addition of new chairs and in some cases the suppression of existing ones, but in general they proposed that in future new chairs should be founded only with the consent of the Crown. They also recommended increased endowments for inadequately supported chairs in all the universities except Glasgow. Since the Copyright Act of 1710 the Scottish universities had enjoyed the privilege of receiving on demand a copy of every published work entered at Stationers' Hall, but as there had been some difficulty in the operation of this provision, the commissioners recommended that it should be commuted for an annual monetary grant. While the commission was still in session the Home Secretary, in July 1829, brought to their notice a proposal to found a new university at Dumfries out of certain funds left by John Crichton of Friar's Carse. It so happened that the matter coincided with the educational expansion in England which culminated in the foundation of University and King's Colleges in London, and the commissioners reported in favour of the scheme. They even drew up a detailed proposal for the composition of the University Court and Senatus Academicus of the new university, recommending that in the first instance only classes in Arts and Divinity should be provided. Nothing, however, came of these proposals, as Parliament was fully occupied with the Reform Bill at the time that the commissioners' report was published, and eventually the funds were diverted elsewhere.

This inaction extended to the other recommendations as well, with the result that university reform was held up for nearly thirty years. In the meantime, it is true, a certain limited amount of parliamentary attention was directed to the Scottish universities. In 1836 Lord Melbourne introduced a bill appointing executive commissions to visit the universities with a view to carrying out the recommendations of the Rosebery Commission but, owing to the opposition of the Church of Scotland and the Town Council of Edinburgh, it was dropped in the following year. While this was in progress fresh commissions were appointed to investigate the affairs of Aberdeen and Glasgow under the respective chairmanships of the Earl of Errol and Viscount Melville. On the failure of the bill the oral evidence of the Rosebery Commission was ordered to be printed in 1837, and in the same year an act of parliament implemented the recommendation regarding the privilege of Stationers' Hall. Each university was to receive compensation based on the estimated extent to which it had previously availed itself of the privilege. This was fixed at an annual sum of £707 for Glasgow, £630 for St. Andrews, £575 for Edinburgh, and £320 for Aberdeen. The Aberdeen commission reported in 1838 and the Glasgow commission in 1839, and in 1840 Lord Melville was again appointed chairman of a Royal Commission on St. Andrews, which sat until 1845. But, by a strange omission, the University of Edinburgh, whose affairs had originally led to the appointment of the first commission, was left to look after itself.

In 1843 the Disruption in the Church of Scotland raised new problems for the Scottish universities. By an act of the Scottish parliament of 1690, confirmed in 1707 by the Act of Security, all principals and professors were required to subscribe to the Westminster Confession and sign the Formula of the Church of Scotland. The measure had been primarily directed against Episcopalians and during the eighteenth century had not been very rigidly enforced, but as the law stood it applied equally to all dissenters. At Edinburgh the majority of the members of the Town Council were adherents of the Free Church, and as early as 1847 they endeavoured to appoint a Free Churchman professor of Hebrew in the University. As a theological chair was involved the Senatus Academicus successfully resisted the appointment in the Court of Session, but three years later, when another Free Churchman was appointed to the chair of moral philosophy, it was decided to take no action as this was a non-theological chair. But the position was manifestly unsatisfactory and was ended in 1853 by an act of parliament 'to regulate admission to the lay chairs in the universities of Scotland'. Under the terms of this measure tests were dispensed with for all chairs except these in the Faculty of Divinity.

The movement for university reform in Scotland received considerable impetus from contemporary efforts in England to introduce reforms into the ancient universities of Oxford and Cambridge. Even more strenuous opposition was encountered there, but in 1850 Royal Commissions under the Bishops of Norwich and Chester were set up to investigate the state of these two universities. Their reports, each of which was published in 1852, led to the Oxford University Act of 1854 and the Cambridge University Act of 1856, under which executive commissions were charged with working out details of the projected reforms. At Edinburgh new difficulties arose between the Senatus Academicus and the Town Council on the question of the recognition of extra-mural teaching for certain purposes. Despite the decision given by the Court of Session in 1829 the Senatus persisted in the belief that the power of making regulations for degrees belonged to them and not to the Town Council. They decided therefore on this occasion to take the matter to the House of Lords, although it entailed going through the preliminary channels once more. In the Court of Session a fresh decision was given against the Senatus in 1850, which was confirmed on appeal in 1852. In 1854 the judgment of the Scottish Courts was upheld by the House of Lords and it was clear that legislation could not be delayed. The Crimean War and the Indian Mutiny caused a temporary postponement and the question of the union of the two Aberdeen colleges was still outstanding.

In 1857, however, a further Royal Commission was appointed to inquire into the state of the Universities of Aberdeen with a view to their union. This commission reported in 1858 and a bill 'to make provision for the better government and discipline of the universities of Scotland and for the union of the two universities and colleges of Aberdeen' was prepared on the basis of the recommendations made. It received the royal assent on 2nd August 1858 and became effective immediately, except that certain provisions were delegated to an executive commission to put into effect. The Universities (Scotland) Act of 1858 is undoubtedly a landmark in the history of the higher education of the country, and it had a profound effect in raising the standard of professional learning in Scotland.

PART III

THE MIDDLE OF THE CENTURY

CHAPTER IV

THE EDUCATION ACT OF 1872

THE Royal Commission appointed to inquire into the schools of Scotland was constituted in August 1864 and consisted in the first instance of 15 members with the Duke of Argyll as chairman. The commission's most important work was done in the sphere of elementary education but its terms of reference included burgh schools, grant-aided schools of any description, 'middle-class' schools which were not in receipt of state grants, training colleges and even such private adventure schools as might be revelant to the inquiry. As a consequence, the commission has been not inaptly compared to the Newcastle, Clarendon and Taunton commissions rolled into one, since these three bodies were required to accomplish a similar task for England and Wales. It is perhaps a rather flattering analogy, in relation to the complexity of the problems to be solved, but the fact remains that the Argyll Commission was responsible for inspiring a comprehensive reorganization of the whole educational system of the country.

As a preliminary measure the commissioners began by taking oral evidence from 38 persons of weight and experience; this they published, together with written evidence from others, in a first report in March 1865. The Commission was then reconstituted, with 18 members, under the same chairman. To help them with the actual work of investigating the existing system of schools, the reconstituted commission appointed five assistant commissioners, Messrs. A. C. Sellar, C. F. Maxwell, J. Greig, T. Harvey and A. Nicolson. In order to take a random sample of the provision of elementary education throughout the country, Sellar and Maxwell were deputed to investigate schools in country districts, Greig and Harvey those in Glasgow, and Nicolson those in the Hebrides. On the basis of their reports the commissioners published their second report, dealing with elementary schools, in 1867.

On the one hand, the commissioners found a statutory system of parochial, side and parliamentary schools which they described as 'established by law, maintained by local assessment, and designed to be commensurate with the educational needs of the country'. On the other hand, they also found a supplementary system (due partly to denominational rivalry but mainly to the deficiencies of the national system) which in practice furnished more than two-thirds of the education in rural districts and practically the whole of that in the towns. In actual statistics a mere 1035 elementary schools out of a total of 4450, less than a quarter, constituted the national system. Even then, the commissioners estimated that of a computed school population of 510,000 some 92,000 were on the roll of no school at all. The 1035 statutory schools comprised 917 parochial, 189 side and 29 parliamentary schools, which accommodated 88,000 out of a total of 312,000 children of school age in rural areas. Of the voluntary schools 880 were undenominational and just over 900 were classed as private adventure schools. The remaining schools comprised 519 Church of Scotland, 202 S.S.P.C.K., 617 Free Church, 74 Episcopalian, 61 Roman Catholic and 45 Presbyterian schools of smaller denominations.

A surprising feature of the investigation, in view of such extensive supplementation of statutory provision by voluntary effort, was the relatively small number of schools that availed themselves of Privy Council grants. Overall, fewer than one third of the total did so. In 1865-6, for instance, of the 1008 statutory parochial and side schools maintained by the heritors only 334 were in receipt of a grant. All the parliamentary schools under the act of 1837 drew the schoolmaster's salary from the Treasury, but only three out of the 29 availed themselves of Privy Council grants for other purposes. Even among the voluntary schools the demand was only moderate, though it varied among the different denominations, the number of schools in question being just over half in the case of the two major Presbyterian churches, two-thirds in the case of the Roman Catholics, and all except one of the schools maintained by the Episcopal church. In spite of this, fees averaging 2½d per week were charged in all these schools, and the assistant commissioners estimated that fees amounting to £70,000 per annum were collected in schools inspected by the Committee of Council alone—a sum as large as that earned from Privy Council grants in the same schools. The commissioners held that the fees charged by the Church of Scotland and Free Church Schools were in some cases too high, but they were against their total abolition, partly on grounds of economy and partly because they genuinely believed that gratuitous education would be a mistake.

It is significant, however, that the commissioners did not think that the Privy Council system either was or could be made into a national system of education. They enumerated under four heads what they personally considered to be the characteristics of a national system. In the first place, there should be some recognized body possessing the legal power both to establish as many national schools as might be required and to prevent unnecessary duplication of effort in any particular area. Secondly, the inhabitants of a district, instead of having to rely on voluntary effort, should be empowered to raise by local taxation such funds as might be required for erecting and maintaining a sufficient number of schools in their area. Thirdly, these schools should be public and national in the sense that every parent should be entitled to claim admission for his child, while reserving the right to object on religious grounds to any part of the instruction given. Fourthly, the inspection of national schools should be undenominational in character. In short, the commissioners were of the opinion that the denominational system as a whole was unnecessary in Scotland. On the other hand, they did not propose to scrap the existing denominational schools. What they had in mind was an extension of the parochial system on its original model, on a scale proportionate to the whole population and without any necessity for throwing aside schools erected by voluntary effort. In other words, they hoped that by a judicious process of improving the parochial schools, taking advantage of existing voluntary schools, modifying the system of Privy Council grants and extending school inspection all schools might be made efficient and come in time to assume a national character.

In the existing state of affairs the principal weakness was manifestly the lack of a central authority. To remedy this the commissioners proposed the establishment of a Board of Education composed of 14 members representing the four universities, the four largest cities, certain counties and the Crown, together with a salaried chairman and secretary. The duties of this Board would, however, be purely local and would not interfere with the jurisdiction of the Committee of Privy Council on Education. The functions to be assigned to the Board were to be such duties as determining the number and character of the schools required in each parish or burgh, incorporating into the national system such existing schools as might seem expedient, authorizing and enforcing the erection of any new schools that might be needed, and ensuring proper maintenance of school buildings and efficient teaching. The commissioners made no recommendation about a uniform local authority but simply proposed that, subject to certain modifications, the existing management of the parochial schools should be retained. They were in favour of abolishing the parochial schoolmaster's traditional *ad vitam aut culpam* tenure of office, and they recommended that the heritors should be obliged to keep their school-houses in a better state of repair. They proposed also that the existing management of the voluntary schools should likewise be retained after their adoption into the national system, but that they should participate in government grants, in return for which they would be subject to government inspection.

The commissioners saw, however, that it would be necessary, particularly in large towns, to make provision for the establishment of additional schools, and therefore recommended a departure from the existing machinery. In this they came near to recommending the creation of a local authority, for within the framework of a national system they proposed over and above the statutory 'parochial' schools and the 'adopted' voluntary schools a third category of 'new' schools. The management of this last class of school was to be vested in a local school committee, elected by the votes of the ratepayers (half and half by owners and occupiers) in rural areas and nominated by the municipality in urban districts. A parochial or adopted school might elect to become a new school by a two-thirds majority of the existing managers, after which it would come under the management of a local school committee. In view of the fact that these proposals would require legislation, the commissioners submitted along with their report a draft bill embodying their recommendations. In it they suggested that the voluntary schools should not be entitled to share in any local rate authorized for educational purposes. The privilege of adoption should be exercised with due discretion and be restricted to denominational schools in existence within two years of the bill becoming law. It was proposed that all adopted schools should satisfy three criteria, namely that they were necessary for the district, that the teaching was efficient and that the school buildings were satisfactory.

The commissioners recommended, further, that every national school should be annually inspected except in respect of religious knowledge (unless by request) and that subject to a conscience clause it should be open to pupils of any denomination. Only national schools would in future share in the parliamentary grant, and in that respect the commissioners showed themselves somewhat lacking in vision, for after the temporary respite that their investigations had given they recommended that the Revised Code should apply to Scottish schools. Only as regards article 4, which introduced an element of class distinction alien to the Scottish tradition by restricting the provision of public education to children whose parents supported themselves by manual labour, did they recommend any modification. To ensure efficiency in teaching they suggested that in future all teachers in national schools should be required to possess a certificate of competency granted either by the Committee of Council or by the university examiners appointed by the Parochial and Burgh Schoolmasters Act of 1861. On due cause shown the proposed Board of Education should have power to suspend or withdraw such certificates. On the question of cost the commissioners reckoned that throughout the country the requisite number of schools could be supplied by a maximum rate of twopence in the pound in rural areas and most towns, and twopence-halfpenny in the Hebrides and in Glasgow and other large towns in which the existing educational provision was least adequate.

No immediate action was taken on the presentation of the report of the Argyll Commission and legislation was delayed, despite two abortive attempts, until 1872. In that year, however, the historic Education (Scotland) Act was successfully piloted through Parliament by the Lord Advocate, and consequently it is sometimes referred to, after the name of its sponsor, as the Young Act. In the meantime Mr. W. E. Forster had secured the passing of the Education Act of 1870 for England and Wales, though it dealt only with elementary education. In consequence of this it is not surprising that although the Scottish Act, based on the Argyll Commission's second and third reports was not restricted in this way, a certain measure of common policy should have characterized the two statutes. It is true that this entailed some modifications in the recommendations made by the Commission in respect of both elementary and middle-class schools, but on the whole the general principles underlying the two reports were put into effect. In view of the existence of previous legislation relating to education in Scotland, the new measure was an act to amend and extend the provisions of the law of Scotland on the subject of education, 'in such manner that the means of procuring efficient education for their children may be furnished and made available to the whole people of Scotland', but it virtually created an entirely new system of education for the country.

For the first time a central authority was set up to coordinate educational resources, although not precisely in the form envisaged by the Argyll Commission. Instead of the purely local Board of Education recommended in their second report, the establishment of a separate Committee of the Privy Council on Education in Scotland was implied in the first section of the act; this was in fact constituted by an order in council dated 9th August 1872. On its executive side it was known as the Scotch Education Department, but for a number of years it did not enjoy an independent existence, for it had to share with the English Committee the same President (the Lord President of the Council), Vice-President (as provided for under the order in council of 25th February 1856) and permanent Secretary (Sir Francis Sandford). The inevitable consequence was a marked tendency towards assimilation of policy in the two countries. As the headquarters of the Scotch Education Department remained in London, a temporary Board of Education for Scotland, consisting of five members to be nominated by the Crown, was also set up to ease the transition from the old order to the new. In section 3 of the act this body was authorized for a period of three years after the passing of the act. It was duly constituted, under the chairmanship of Sir John Don-Wauchope, Bart., by an order in council of 10th October 1872, but its powers were continued finally until 1878. During the six years of its existence the Board of Education published an annual report and, being centred in Edinburgh, undoubtedly exerted a highly beneficial influence on Scottish education at a critical moment in the history of its development.

The act also introduced a local authority to superintend what were henceforth to be known as 'public' schools, though in this it departed from the general tenor of the commission's recommendations for the management of existing schools. This was the triennially elected school board which, as in England, was to have jurisdiction over an area in general coterminous with a burgh or a civil parish. There was this difference, however, that whereas the act of 1870 made the election of school boards in England and Wales merely permissive, the eighth section of the Scottish act of 1872 laid down that a school board should be elected for every parish or burgh in Scotland within twelve months of the passing of the act. The country was thus divided into 984 school districts, but it occasionally happened that there was no school situated within a particular district. The consequence was the curious paradox that in England there were districts with schools but no school boards and in Scotland a number of districts with school boards but no schools. The act, however, did permit the union of two or more school boards under certain circumstances, and the original number was gradually, though only slightly, reduced. Thus the number of school boards had been reduced to 981 (923 parish and 58 burgh boards) by 1888, to 978 (seven of which were still without schools) by 1901, and to 967 by 1911. The composition of these boards varied from five to fifteen members, as determined for each parish and burgh by the Board of Education for Scotland, and under the twenty-third and twenty-fourth sections of the act the management of every parochial and burgh school was transferred to the appropriate school board. Under section 38 denominational schools might also be transferred voluntarily, but transfer was not made obligatory for the continuance of state-aid to such schools.

In fact, however, apart from the relatively few Roman Catholic and Episcopal schools which were more strictly sectarian than other church schools, the great majority of voluntary schools were transferred to the school boards within the next year or two. The ease with which this was effected is no doubt attributable to the avoidance of explicit reference to the religious question in the text of the act. The preamble did allude to the custom of giving religious instruction in the public schools of Scotland to children whose parents did not object to it, and without prejudice to those who elected that their children should not receive such instruction, with an expression that the *status quo* should be maintained by the managers of public schools. To this end a conscience clause was inserted in section 68, which authorized the withdrawal of any child from instruction in religion or any religious observance in a public school and, no doubt to avoid dislocation of the time-table, limited the time during which this instruction might be given to the beginning or the end of the school day. It was not, however, found necessary, as in England, to insert a Cowper-Temple clause forbidding the teaching of any religious catechism or formulary distinctive of a particular denomination in a rate-aided school.

Another indication that the sectarian spirit was less intransigent in Scotland is to be found in the fact that the period of grace for 'filling the gaps' was made in favour of the new school boards and not, as in England, of the voluntary religious bodies. Where a deficiency of school accommodation was discovered in any district, the school board was permitted to make an application to the Scotch Education Department for a building grant any time before 31st December 1873. Previous experience of a statutory system of education, however imperfect, made a greater measure of compulsion practicable than in England, and every parent was required to provide elementary education in reading, writing and arithmetic for his children while they were between five and thirteen years of age. No discretion in the matter was left to individual school boards, as was the case in England, and all school boards were further required to appoint a school attendance officer. No authority was, however, given to the Department to exert pressure on any school board which might prove negligent in enforcing its power of compulsion. The school boards were required to maintain and keep efficient all schools under their management and to fix the fees to be paid for attendance at each such school.

To modern ways of thinking a curious feature of the act was that, while introducing compulsory attendance, it did not also make schooling free. There was undoubtedly something anomalous in this, and some highland school boards interpreted section 53, dealing with the procedure for collecting and disposing of school fees, as being merely permissive and consequently charged none. In cases of inability to pay the fees demanded, the English act of 1870 had made provision for partial or total remission, but under the Scottish act any parent who was unable to meet his obligations was required to apply for assistance to the parochial board of his parish or burgh. Nor was any limit to the amount that might be charged in the way of fees laid down in the Scottish act, whereas a maximum of ninepence per week was stipulated in the English act. From the beginning, however, the Scotch Education Department ruled that the ordinary payments in respect of instruction should not exceed ninepence a week from each child, and this decision was later given statutory authority by the English Elementary Education Act of 1876. In the fifty-third section of this act, generally called Lord Sandon's Act, it was laid down that the conditions to be fulfilled by schools to obtain an annual parliamentary grant should apply to Scotland, and of these one was that the fees charged in grant-earning schools should be limited to ninepence a week.

The school boards were given the right of appointing all the teachers in the schools under their management, except where teachers had held office before the passing of the act. These were confirmed in their existing appointments, but powers of dismissal under the Parochial and Burgh Schoolmasters Act of 1861 were now to be vested in the school boards and were extended to include incompetence and inefficiency as well as immorality and cruelty. The act required that in future all those appointed to the office of principal teacher should hold a certificate of competency, but did not make it obligatory on all teachers in public schools, as had been recommended by the Argyll Commission. Under section 57 the Scotch Education Department was instructed to make regulations from time to time for the granting of such certificates. School boards were permitted at their discretion to pay retiring allowances to teachers who had obtained permission to resign their posts.

To meet the financial requirements imposed by the act, a school fund was to be established in connection with every school board and any deficiency was to be met by a special 'school-rate' authorized under section 44. The school boards were also given powers for borrowing money for necessary capital expenditure on the security of the rates. Thus, the school fund was to consist of the parliamentary grant, any money raised by loan in this manner, and such other funds as were not specially appropriated to any particular purpose. This did not, however, include school fees, which were to be separately accounted for and might be divided among the teachers of the school from which they were derived, as the school board should determine. All public schools were made subject to inspection by any of H.M. Inspectors but religious instruction was exempted from this requirement. Every school subject to inspection and in receipt of public money was required to open its doors to children of all denominations. In this way, the four characteristics of a national system of education, as envisaged by the members of the Argyll Commission, were more or less realized in practice. The act also dealt with the middle-class schools discussed in the commissioners' final report, but its provisions under that head will be treated separately.

In 1873 the Scotch Education Department issued its first code, at length enforcing the principle of payment by results which had been temporarily suspended in 1864. In the interval, however, experience had modified some of its most objectionable features and some allowance was now made for intelligent and grammatical knowledge of the reading-material in the lower standards, and for a creditable showing in history and geography in the upper standards. A graduated bonus was even given for organization and discipline, and to fulfil its duty in maintaining the standard of education previously existing in the public schools of Scotland, the Department offered grants for passes in 'specific subjects' by pupils who had completed the sixth standard. Such additional studies had been first recognized by the English code in 1867 to promote the teaching of a wider variety of subjects and to encourage pupil teachers to remain at school. In Scotland custom required that at least the traditional university subjects of Latin, Greek and mathematics should be included in the approved list of specific subjects, but in addition to these the Department also recognized ten others for grant-earning purposes. Three of these were linguistic in nature, namely English, French and German, and the remaining seven were scientific, viz. mechanics, light and heat, magnetism and electricity, physical geography, chemistry, botany and animal physiology. In each of the thirteen subjects the scheme envisaged a three-year course graduated in three stages, and it permitted pupils from standards IV to VI to be presented for examination in not more than two of them, while those above the sixth standard might be presented in three specific subjects.

Unfortunately, the method of payment was likely to lead to anomalies, since the grant in each subject and at each level was fixed at the uniform figure of 4/- per pass. It was difficult, for instance, to equate the standard among so heterogeneous a collection of subjects, and Scottish opinion could hardly be expected to accept a year's teaching of physiology as being equivalent to one of Greek. Moreover, the system was prone to encourage smatterings of learning, since it was financially more profitable to teach many pupils at the first stage of several subjects than to persevere with a few to the higher stages of a more limited number. It was felt too—and, as events proved, rightly—that the policy of payment by results in the elementary subjects would react unfavourably on the teaching of the specific subjects by its exacting demands on the efforts of the teacher.

As a result of widespread criticism the position was reviewed after a few years by the commissioners appointed in terms of the Endowed Institutions (Scotland) Act of

1878. As part of their duties they were required, in the eleventh section of the act, to inquire into the conditions according to which the parliamentary grant for public education in Scotland might be most advantageously distributed for the purpose of promoting education in the higher branches of knowledge in public and state-aided schools, especially in districts where there were no higher class public schools. A second Education (Scotland) Act was passed in the same year, sometimes known as Lord Watson's Act, but as regards elementary education its provisions were largely procedural, relating chiefly to such technicalities as resignations of members of school boards, compulsory purchase of school sites, the method of paying the school rate by the parochial board and similar matters.

CHAPTER V

SECONDARY EDUCATION 1861-1878

In their third report, published in 1868, the Argyll Commission dealt with burgh and middle-class schools. Two of the assistant commissioners, Messrs. Harvey and Sellar, had been detailed to investigate the state of secondary education throughout the country, and consequently the commissioners' report was supplemented by a general report and special reports on the existing institutions, compiled by them. In conjunction with the Schools Inquiry Commission under Lord Taunton which was at that time sitting in London, the Argyll Commission appointed an assistant commissioner, the Rev. James Fraser, afterwards Bishop of Manchester, to investigate educational provision in Canada and America, and a report by him was jointly published for the two commissions in the same year. The commissioners had already in their second report called attention to the fact that, except in the case of smaller burghs which formed part of rural parishes, no legislative provision existed for the establishment and maintenance of schools in the seventy-nine royal burghs of Scotland.

When the assistant commissioners came to investigate the actual position, however, they found that in all but three of them (Kinghorn, Oban and Portobello) some kind of educational provision had in fact been made. In forty of the royal burghs, however, there was no burgh school properly so-called, and of a total of eighty-two 'middle-class schools' only thirty-two were burgh schools, while nine were mixed burgh and parochial schools, eighteen simply parochial schools and twenty-three technically academies. In addition to the provision of such schools in burghs, the commissioners found four similar schools situated outside the areas of burghs and they also investigated eleven private schools of the same category, though specifying only three of these by name. As regards the level of the instruction provided, they adopted three classifications, viz. purely elementary, mixed elementary and secondary, and definitely higher than elementary. They concluded that in the larger burghs the great majority belonged to the second of these classes, while in only two, Aberdeen and Edinburgh, were there any belonging to the third class. Indeed, they professed to find 'but six schools in Scotland to which the designation of secondary schools is applicable'. They comprised four public schools in burghs (the Old and New Grammar Schools in Aberdeen, and the Academy and Royal High School in Edinburgh), one public school outside the area of a burgh (Trinity College, Glenalmond) and one private school (the Aberdeen Gymnasium). All the others were said to 'present a confusion of infant, primary and elementary schools combined in one'.

Shortly before the investigation carried out by Harvey and Sellar, Mr. D. R. Fearon had been sent as assistant commissioner by the Schools Inquiry Commission to institute a comparison between the Scottish burgh schools and the endowed schools of England. As an inspector of schools in England, Fearon was greatly impressed by the educational zeal of the nine burgh and seven other Scottish schools which he visited in the spring of 1866. The picture he paints of the state of secondary education in Scotland, though admittedly based only on a sample, is considerably more enthusiastic than the account given by Harvey and Sellar, who began operations later in the same year. One particular point of difference was the co-educational character of many of the burgh schools, which led Fearon to conclude that a mixture of the sexes resulted in mutual benefit. Harvey and Sellar, on the other hand, while admitting that intellectually the arrangement had much to recommend it, dissented on social grounds, but the commissioners were not unanimous in upholding their view on this point. In general, however, the commissioners accepted the criticisms directed against the existing system by their two deputies and incorporated in their report recommendations that were designed to improve the state of the schools.

Thus, Harvey and Sellar deprecated the customary *ad vitam aut culpam* tenure of office and the low teacher-pupil ratio as productive of inefficiency. They expressed the opinion that the pupils came too late and left too early, that the hours of work were excessive, and that in comparison with English schools physical education was neglected. They drew attention to the fact that whereas 71% of the teachers in burgh schools had had a university education, only 36% were graduates, and concluded from that that a degree was not in such universal demand as would seem desirable. They commented adversely on school buildings by classifying 40% of them as indifferent or worse. Playgrounds were not adapted for games, repairs were carried out in too economical a spirit and altogether the most notable feature of the schools was their lack of endowments. To the credit of the schools, however, they believed that the accommodation provided was sufficient to meet the demand, that the personal relations between teacher and pupil were highly satisfactory, and that so far as it went the education given was not only sound but an adequate preparation for the Scottish universities.

On the basis of these views, the commissioners were inclined to an optimistic opinion of the educational situation in the country, and refrained from making any sweeping recommendations with regard to the burgh and middle-class schools. By 'middle-class' schools they understood those in which the general education of the pupils ended at their sixteenth year, and from the returns made they estimated that more than two-thirds of the middle-class population of Scotland was receiving its education in the schools under investigation. In terms of statistics this meant 1 in 140 of the whole population if private schools were included, but only 1 in 205 if only public secondary schools were taken into account. Even then, the latter figure compared with 1 in 249 in Prussia, 1 in 570 in France and 1 in 1300 in England. The statistics relating to university education were equally favourable to Scotland, where a ratio of 1 in 1000 compared with 1 in 2600 in Germany and 1 in 5800 in England. With regard to the university figures, the commissioners nevertheless remarked that only 42% of the students proceeded directly from burgh and middle-class schools. They recognized the importance of preserving the traditional connection between the parochial schools and the universities, and pointed out that in dealing with Scottish education that fact was of vital importance. As originally conceived in the First Book of Discipline, the theory of the Scottish educational system was not only to supply every member of the community with the elements of education but to enable him to pass to the university through the burgh school or even directly from the parish school.

To increase efficiency in the burgh schools, the commissioners recommended a system of superannuation by means of government grants as a relief against sickness or old age, and they also advocated the extension of central grants to cover necessary repairs to the buildings of burgh schools. In return for these sums the burgh schools should be subject to annual inspection by one of H.M. Inspectors as regards both efficiency of teaching and the state of the fabric. It would also be desirable to abolish the old *ad vitam aut culpam* tenure of office enjoyed by masters and their assistants in the burgh schools, although not without some safeguard against capricious dismissal by the employing authority. To preserve the traditional avenue from the parochial school to the university, the commissioners recommended that in districts where a want of burgh schools was known to exist special grants to encourage the teaching of the higher branches should be made to the parish schools, even if such an arrangement should entail additional standards above those recognized by the Revised Code. Apart from these very minor subventions the commissioners advocated that no further grants of public money should be made to the burgh schools, and, as in the case of the parish schools, they gave proof of their confidence in the traditional system by recommending that no alteration should be made in the existing management.

In conclusion, the commissioners put forward a recommendation relating to a class of school which they took no steps to have examined but simply circularized for information. This was the endowed hospital, which in a sense corresponded to the 'Public School' of England, though the residential system had never taken firm root in Scottish esteem. From returns received from eleven endowed hospitals the commissioners reached the conclusion that while the majority of these institutions furnished 'what may be called a liberal education, including Latin, Greek and mathematics', the educational expenditure involved in the process was disproportionately high as compared with that of the burgh schools. The expenditure per pupil ranged from £4 16/- to £12 17/- as against an average of £3 11/6 per annum in the burgh schools. Costs of maintenance per pupil were correspondingly high, although in this case no direct comparison could be made, but on both counts George Watson's Hospital, under the management of the Merchant Company of Edinburgh, was singled out for special mention.

The commissioners suggested that some inquiry might

be made to ascertain whether more economy might not be introduced into the administration of hospitals in general, and for their own part implied that the funds might be put to better use in establishing efficient day schools charging moderate fees, particularly in large towns where working class parents experienced greater difficulty in securing a good education for their children at a reasonable cost than those in rural areas. They recommended accordingly that hospital statutes should be examined with the purpose of making, subject to parliamentary sanction, such necessary alterations in them as would ensure an extension of their educational provision. Of all the recommendations made by the commissioners this last was in some ways the most far-reaching in its repercussions on the secondary education of the country. Nor were its effects long delayed in making themselves felt, for on 3rd April 1868 at a meeting of the governors of George Watson's Hospital it was resolved to request the education committee to consider the existing course of study in relation to the subsequent careers of the hospital pupils and to 'invite one or more experienced gentlemen' to examine the various classes and test the teaching given in the hospital.

In response to the request made by the governors it was decided to approach the Secretary of the Education Committee of the Church of Scotland, Mr. (later Professor) S. S. Laurie, since he was 'a gentleman possessed of such experience and independence of character that the governors might thoroughly rely on receiving from him an impartial and candid report of the real state of the present management of the hospital'. Events proved that the choice was indeed a judicious one, and Laurie's mandate was extended to include, in addition to the original commitment, Daniel Stewart's Hospital, the Merchant Maiden Hospital and a free school for boys carried on in association with James Gillespie's Hospital, which was actually an asylum for old people. The management of all four institutions was in the hands of the Merchant Company of Edinburgh, and Laurie produced a detailed report on each as well as a general report on hospital training. The result, aptly described as 'a report which is a classic as far as the hospital system is concerned', was submitted to the Merchant Company in June 1868. Laurie concurred with the Argyll Commission's strictures on the cost of hospital education but was careful both to absolve the Merchant Company from any charge of mismanagement and to acquit its servants of any imputation of inefficiency. None the less he condemned the hospital system as a whole. 'I have been led,' he said, 'to conclusions even much larger and more antagonistic to the present constitution of things than I have felt myself at liberty here to record.'

Neither intellectually nor morally did he consider the system a wholesome one, and summed up its wants under the heads of moral and intellectual ventilation, self-dependence and family life. Somewhat to his own surprise he found the evils of the hospital system to be 'even more conspicuous among girls than among boys'. Accordingly, he advocated the breaking up of what he called the monastic character of these institutions, either by converting them into boarding establishments pure and simple and sending the foundationers to outside schools for their education, or alternatively by converting the hospitals into fee-paying day schools (as suggested by the Argyll Commission) and boarding out the foundationers with relatives or friends. Such drastic action could not, of course, be accomplished without legislation, but the governors of George Watson's Hospital approved the report on general principles and the Merchant Company pressed the Lord Advocate to introduce a bill. It so happened that in England the report of the Taunton Commission was in process of leading up to a bill in connection with the endowed grammar schools about the same time, and it culminated in the Endowed Schools Act of 1869, which permitted certain changes in the statutes governing grammar school foundations. In July of the same year an Endowed Institutions (Scotland) Act was also passed, but it proved in practice to be a very limited piece of legislation.

Under this act the governing bodies of endowed institutions might apply to the Home Secretary for a provisional order to make certain approved alterations to the conditions of the trust-deed of their foundation, with a view to increasing its educational usefulness. The Edinburgh Merchant Company was the first body to avail itself of the provisions of the act, and in 1870 succeeded in obtaining the necessary provisional order to convert Daniel Stewart's and the Merchant Maiden hospitals into fee-paying day schools for each of the sexes. On the same model George Watson's Hospital was converted into a double collegiate school for either sex, and in the case of James Gillespie's Hospital the funds of free school and hospital were united to provide a larger and better equipped elementary school. The only other endowment which was able to take advantage of the act was Bathgate Academy, which likewise obtained a provisional order to amend its trust-deed in the same year.

Opposition among certain sections of the teaching profession was aroused, and when in 1871 the governors of George Heriot's Hospital endeavoured to follow suit permission was refused. No further schemes under the provisions of the act were entertained owing to inadequate drafting in its terms. Nevertheless, the act, though largely abortive, had the effect of directing attention to the need for amending the terms of educational trusts and of influencing public opinion against the founding of any further hospitals. Thus in 1870 the trustees of the funds left in 1836 by Sir William Fettes abandoned the idea of erecting a hospital in favour of a public boarding school on the model of Rugby or Harrow. In time, too, the majority of the remaining hospitals were converted under subsequent legislation into endowed secondary schools of a type similar to those of the Merchant Company, which thus had an important influence on the development of specifically secondary education in Scottish schools.

In the meantime the Education (Scotland) Act of 1872 also introduced significant changes into the previously existing system of middle-class schools, although not altogether along the lines recommended by the Argyll Commission. As in the case of the parochial schools, the management of burgh schools was transferred from their former patrons, the Town Council and magistrates, to the new school boards. A burgh school was defined in the first section of the act as one to which the term was legally applicable whether called an academy, a high school or a grammar school. Such schools, like purely elementary schools, became 'public schools' and were subject to the same general requirements imposed on institutions sharing in parliamentary grants and the school rate. In section 67 of the act the Department was instructed to take due care, in framing its minutes, that the standard of education previously existing in the public schools should not be lowered but as far as possible be maintained. By this means it was hoped that the secondary education provided in the burgh schools and the advanced instruction given in the parochial schools would be safeguarded, but there can be little doubt that the policy of putting secondary schools on the same footing as elementary ones was unfortunate. Despite the fact that Scottish tradition had always been against rigid demarcation of the two types of school, the act served only to encourage an assimilating influence which was prejudicial to the development of a real system of secondary education in the country as a whole.

A rather faint-hearted attempt to forestall this tendency was made, it is true, in the sixty-second section of the act, by which a special (not very happily named) 'higher class' public school was granted recognition. Schools of this type were exempted from some of the provisions affecting all other public schools. The criterion by which they were to be recognized as such was that the education given in them did not consist chiefly of elementary instruction in reading, writing and arithmetic but of the higher branches of knowledge such as the classics, modern languages, mathematics and science. In schedule C of the act eleven burgh schools, situated respectively in Aberdeen, Ayr, Dumfries, Edinburgh, Elgin, Glasgow, Haddington, Montrose, Paisley, Perth and Stirling, were specified as satisfying this requirement. School boards were, however, authorized subject to Departmental approval to resolve that any other burgh school under their management should be deemed a higher class public school. This concession was extended even to parish school boards in respect of parochial schools under their management, provided instruction in the higher branches of knowledge was given to such an extent and to such a number of pupils that the school could not reasonably be regarded as chiefly an elementary one.

There was, however, a powerful deterrent which militated against widespread acceptance of the opportunity of up-grading other public schools to the status of higher class public schools, namely the financial sacrifice entailed. Not only were such schools ineligible for state grants but, though placed under the jurisdiction of school boards, they were also precluded from sharing in the local school-rate. Hence, by 1888 the original number had increased only to 20 higher class public schools throughout the country, but after 1892 the financial position improved and in 1901 the number had risen to a total of 32 schools of this class. Thus deprived of both state and local aid, the higher class public schools had to depend on three slender sources of income: endowments, if any, pupils' fees, and contributions from the 'common good' of the burgh in which they were situated. The act did do something to regulate the latter two sources by giving them statutory authority. By section 46 town councils were required to continue paying the same amount out of the common good as had been their custom before the passing of the act. Section 62 decreed that all fees should be paid into a common fund for distribution among the teachers of the particular school, as should be determined by the school board, but it allowed the teachers themselves to fix at three-yearly intervals the actual amount to be charged for attendance at their school, subject to the approval of the school board. The former practice whereby teachers had simply pocketed the fees paid by the pupils they personally taught was thus abolished, although it continued in the universities until the act of 1889.

The higher class public schools were allowed, on the other hand, a much greater degree of independence than other schools under the management of school boards. Since they were to be specifically managed with a view to promoting the higher education of the country, the act laid down that so far as practicable they should be relieved of the necessity of giving elementary instruction in reading, writing and arithmetic to young children. Teachers employed in them were exempted from examination by the Department and the question of fixing qualifications was left to the discretion of the individual school boards, with the proviso that only professors in the Scottish universities or teachers of distinction in existing higher class public schools should act as examiners. The necessary academic standing of those appointed was thus ensured but no provision was made for testing their professional fitness. Finally, these schools were not to be subject to ordinary inspection by H.M. Inspectors, although they were required to be examined annually in the higher branches of knowledge which were taught in them. For this purpose the school boards were instructed to employ special examiners and to pay the expenses of examination out of the school fund. Extensions to existing buildings and the cost of erecting new ones might also be a charge on the school fund, but these were the only instances in which school boards were authorized to spend ratepayers' money on higher class public schools.

It should perhaps be pointed out, to the credit of school boards, that since there was no restriction on the type of education that might be provided in other schools under their management, except for the limits imposed by the code, there was little point in having a school specifically labelled a higher class public school at such financial disadvantage. The chief drawback was simply that such schools would not be relieved of the necessity of providing elementary instruction as well. Nor should it be overlooked that secondary schools which were not legally burgh schools, e.g. subscription academies, endowed institutions and private schools, remained unaffected by the act and continued to play an important part in the development of purely secondary education. Although not enjoying official recognition, they became generically known as 'higher class schools', and some of them were financially in a more privileged position than their 'public' counterparts. It is true that various circumstances compelled a few of those in the first-mentioned category to lose their independent status by coming in time under the management of school boards, but those in the second category were greatly strengthened by the reform of endowments which was set afoot by the activity of the Argyll Commission and the Merchant Company of Edinburgh.

Following upon the ill-fated act of 1869, a Royal Commission was set up, little more than a month after the passing of the Education (Scotland) Act of 1872, to inquire into all educational endowments in Scotland. The chairman was Sir Thomas Edward Colebrooke, Bart., and the secretary the energetic and capable Simon S. Laurie. The commission's terms of reference included inquiry into the nature and amount of all educational endowments, investigation of the administration and management of any institutions supported by them, and recommendation of any changes which might increase the usefulness and efficiency of such endowments. In comparison with England the amount of money involved was trifling, but since no previous attempt had been made to assess Scottish educational endowments collectively, the task proved formidable and occupied the commission for nearly three years. Eventually, however, it presented its third and final report, in February 1875, and estimated the annual revenue from educational endowments at approximately £175,000. This was exclusive of some £22,000 which had been acquired by the universities since 1808, previous university endowments having been investigated by the executive commission appointed under the Universities (Scotland) Act of 1858.

The commissioners classified the endowments with which they had to deal under five heads. Firstly, the largest item consisted of 'hospital' endowments, amounting to nearly £80,000 of annual revenue. Secondly, there were what they called 'school' endowments, amounting to some £60,000, of which more than two-thirds was mainly in connection with schools providing chiefly elementary instruction and the rest mainly in connection with schools providing chiefly higher instruction. Thirdly, they estimated that there were 'general' endowments, not appropriated to any particular institution, yielding some £17,000 annually. Of these the three most important were the Dick, Milne and Philp Bequests, which respectively provided about £5,000, £2,000 and £3,000 yearly. The income from the Dick Bequest was devoted to supplementing the statutory salaries of the parish schoolmasters in the counties of Aberdeen, Banff and Moray, and by a system of graduated payments, depending upon merit, excellent results were obtained. The Milne Bequest was somewhat similar in intention but was confined in its operation to Aberdeenshire, and the payments were not graduated. The sum of £20 was paid to the most deserving parish schoolmasters in the county, in return for which they were required in each case to educate free of charge twenty-five poor children who could not otherwise afford to pay for their education. The Philp Bequest operated in certain towns and parishes in the south of Fife for the purpose of educating poor children in the district, but in this instance the trustees used the money for building schools and maintaining teachers of their own. Fourthly, there were 'mixed' endowments, which were partly charitable and partly educational in nature and contributed some £18,500 applicable yearly to educational purposes. Lastly, the university endowments comprised over £8,000 for the endowment of chairs, over £7,000 in fellowships, scholarships and prizes, and over £6,500 in entrance bursaries.

In their recommendations under the head of hospital endowments the commissioners fully endorsed the unfavourable criticism to which the system had previously been subjected. Altogether they enumerated twenty-six institutions of this category, but the total included the three Merchant Company hospitals which had already been reformed, Fettes College, which never became a proper hospital, and some two or three others of lesser importance which were partly public day schools. Few of them were large, and outside Edinburgh the only important hospitals were Gordon's in Aberdeen, and Morgan's in Dundee. Like Laurie, their secretary, the commissioners recommended that the foundationers should be boarded out and the hospitals thrown open to all as day schools. They implied that the instruction given in them, while adapted to the circumstances of the locality, should be more advanced, and that, where practicable, the foundationers should attend public elementary schools in the first instance. The number of charity foundationers should be reduced and in suitable cases they should be made to contribute towards their own maintenance. A considerable proportion of places should be available by competition to boys who had already completed a course of primary instruction.

As for the second class of endowments, the commissioners recommended that those in connection with elementary schools should generally be applied so as to promote advanced instruction in the school and to encourage promising pupils to prolong their school life. To a moderate extent they should continue to assist in providing free elementary education in necessitous cases, but some part at least, particularly where rates were low, should be applied to increasing the efficiency of the school by raising the standard of education. Endowments under this head for higher instruction should be utilized either for directly aiding secondary schools, such as the higher class public schools, or for establishing bursaries to be held at such schools as the reward of merit. Indeed, inasmuch as elementary, but not secondary, schools had already been provided for by legislation, the commissioners advocated that where any surplus remained from elementary school endowments it should be applied to the same purpose.

With regard to mixed endowments, they recommended that the proportions to be set aside for charity and education respectively should be clearly defined, and that in cases where purely charitable funds had been destined for purposes rendered unsuitable through change of circumstances permission should be given to apply them to education. Finally, with regard to university endowments, the commissioners suggested that bursaries in public hands should be made open to competition, that bursaries in private patronage of less than £10 annual value should be combined to provide a reasonable sum and be open to competition, and that for all other private bursaries locally restricted the universities should be allowed to prescribe a standard of attainment, in the absence of which in any one year the particular bursary should be competitive.

To these specific recommendations the commissioners added some of a more general nature. All endowments should be relieved of restrictions in favour of particular names, and restrictions in favour of those connected with the founder's family should be limited by statute. All endowed institutions should be periodically inspected by examiners appointed by the Department or the universities and their accounts should be annually audited. A public register of educational endowments should be compiled and, with regard to governing bodies, power should be given to modify the constitution of trusts where there were too few or too many trustees. In the reconstitution of such trusts adequate representation should be given to local interests, except where a considerable district or secondary education was concerned; in these cases the governing body should, on the contrary, be partly composed of members independent of local influence. Powers should be given to combine trusts, to transfer them to school boards with the approval of the trustees, and to relieve them of denominational restrictions on beneficiaries and teachers alike.

The commissioners were concerned with the want of an administrative body in Scotland to implement the reforms suggested, corresponding to the Charity Commission in England. The latter had been constituted in 1853 for the purpose of conducting inquiries into the conditions and management of charities, and in 1860 had been granted certain judicial powers. To meet the situation, they recommended that an act should be passed conferring the necessary powers on an executive commission, and that at the same time extended powers of dealing with trusts should also be granted to the Court of Session. As a consequence, a second Endowed Institutions (Scotland) Act was passed in 1878; it was designed to remedy the defects of its predecessor in 1869 and authorized the appointment of seven commissioners to carry out its terms. Accordingly, a Royal Commission, which remained in being until 1881, was at once appointed under the chairmanship of Lord Moncrieff, but its effectiveness was greatly hampered by the permissive nature of the statute, which again left the initiative in the hands of governing bodies.

Lord Watson's Act of the same year (1878), already referred to under elementary education, also offered slight concessions to secondary education. The main provision was that by section 18 a school board having the management of a higher class public school should in future maintain the building out of the school fund in the same manner as that of any other school under its management. Permission was also given, in the event of the statutory sources of revenue being insufficient, for a board to apply to the Department for leave to defray any other expenses for the promotion of efficient education in such a school. Unfortunately, however, this was not held to apply to teachers' salaries, and so small advantage could be taken of it. Sections 19 and 20 of the same act permitted the Department to undertake inspection of higher class schools when requested to do so. If under a school board, the inspection of such a school would be carried out free of cost and might serve in place of the statutory annual examination required under the act of 1872. Otherwise, the managing authority must undertake to bear the expense of the examination as determined by the Department.

CHAPTER VI

THE UNIVERSITIES FROM 1858 TO 1889

THE Universities (Scotland) Act of 1858 largely remodelled the Scottish universities and assimilated their constitutions along the lines suggested in the Rosebery Commission's report of 1831. A number of important matters, including the actual union of the two Aberdeen colleges, were left in the hands of the executive commission set up under section 14 of the act. This commission was composed of twelve members and was presided over by the Lord Justice Clerk, John Inglis, afterwards Chancellor of Edinburgh University. It remained in being until the end of 1862 and was empowered to issue ordinances which, once approved by the Queen in Council, could afterwards only be altered with the consent of the Chancellor of the University and the sanction of the Privy Council. In section 1 of the act it was laid down that on and after a date to be appointed by the commission, King's College and Marischal College should be united into one university to be known as the University of Aberdeen; this was put into effect on 15th September 1860.

In section 7 of the act the two-chamber government proposed by the commission of 1826-30 was introduced in all the universities by the institution of a University Court in addition to the existing Senatus Academicus. There were certain modifications, however, for greater powers than those recommended were vested in the Senatus Academicus, which in each university was to consist of the

Principal and all the professors. In addition to superintending and regulating teaching and discipline, this body was charged with administering the property and revenues of the university. The special case of Edinburgh was overlooked in the act, and a special measure, known as the Edinburgh University Property Arrangement Act, was required in 1861 to transfer the university buildings and funds from the Town Council to the Senatus Academicus. The duties of the University Court established in each university included the power of reviewing all decisions of the Senatus Academicus, effecting improvements in internal arrangements, fixing and regulating fees, and exercising a general control over the financial affairs of the university. The appointment of professors, except in cases where chairs were under special patronage, was also vested in the University Court, with the exception of Edinburgh, where a compromise was effected. Previously the appointment of the Principal and the majority of the professors at Edinburgh had been in the hands of the Town Council, and the Rosebery Commission had recommended that this arrangement should continue. For a number of reasons, however, it was found expedient to make the appointing body less unwieldy and to give the University Court some representation on it. Accordingly, in section 13 of the act the patronage of the principalship and the existing professorships was vested in seven curators of patronage. Of these the Town Council was to elect four, and the University Court three, to remain in office for a period of three years. The Town Council thus retained the major control in making appointments.

In addition to the Senatus Academicus and the University Court, the act introduced in each university an advisory body called the General Council. There was no specific recommendation for this innovation in the report of the Rosebery Commission, although graduates had been associated with professors in the election of certain university officers in some of their proposals for reform. It was in fact a deliberate attempt to stimulate the practice of graduation by allowing a measure of control to graduates in the affairs of their university. The control allowed was admittedly somewhat indirect, for the act laid down that the General Council of each university should meet twice yearly to take into consideration all questions affecting the well-being and prosperity of the university and to make representations on such matters to the University Court. The latter was not bound, however, to take action on the representations made.

The members of the General Council were to be the Chancellor, the members of the University Court, the professors, and all Masters of Arts and Doctors of Medicine who had regularly attended classes in the university for four complete sessions. As a special concession to the general lapse in the practice of graduating which had previously been characteristic of most of the universities, those who had before the passing of the act put in the required attendance, even without graduating, were granted an indulgence. They might within three years apply to the executive commission appointed under the act to have their names registered as members of the General Council, provided that they had spent at least two of the four sessions as matriculated students in the Faculty of Arts. The General Council was given the right of nominating an assessor on the University Court and of electing the Chancellor. The latter was to hold office for life, to act as chairman at meetings of the General Council and to preside at graduation ceremonials. He was empowered to appoint a Vice-Chancellor for the sole purpose of conferring degrees in his absence. Though no restriction in choice was laid down, it was customary from the first for Chancellors in all the universities to nominate the Principal to this office, and the tradition is never departed from. At Edinburgh, where the office did not already exist, it was enacted that in time coming there should be a Chancellor.

In all the universities the office of Rector was also assimilated and his term of office fixed at three years. The right of election was given to the matriculated students of each university, although details of the actual manner of voting were left to the commission to settle. In the universities of Glasgow, Aberdeen and Edinburgh the principalship was declared to be dissociated from any chair of theology and might in future be held by a layman. Previously it had been customary to regard the Principal as a professor of Divinity and invariably to appoint an ordained minister to that office, even in the case of Marischal College, Aberdeen, whose foundation-charter specifically allowed of a layman. The Scottish universities had all originally been colleges of Arts and Theology, although later at St. Andrews the Nova Fundatio of 1579 had limited the teaching of theology to St. Mary's College, which was largely an autonomous body. In that case it was clearly outside the jurisdiction of Principals of other colleges, which in consequence might be presumed at liberty to appoint laymen. Yet both at St. Salvator's and St. Leonard's, and subsequently at the United College, the person appointed was always an ecclesiastic until Sir David Brewster became Principal of the United College in 1838. Under section 3 of the act the University of Edinburgh immediately availed itself of the opportunity of appointing a layman as Principal, and the same practice, once inaugurated, was continued at the United College, St. Andrews. But at Glasgow and Aberdeen the clerical tradition died hard and, apart from Sir William Geddes at Aberdeen (1885-1900), no lay Principal was appointed for more than fifty years after the passing of the act.

The University Court was constituted very much along the lines proposed by the Rosebery Commission. It consisted of the Rector as chairman, the Principal (at St. Andrews the Senior Principal only, and not both) as member *ex officio*, and four assessors to be nominated respectively by the Chancellor, Rector, General Council and Senatus Academicus in each university. The Rector's Assessor was limited to three years in office, while the remaining assessors were to be nominated for a period of four years, and all Principals and professors were excluded from serving as assessors except as representatives of the Senatus Academicus. This basic number of six was increased in the case of Glasgow by one member, the Dean of Faculties annually elected by the Senatus Academicus, and at Edinburgh by two additional members, the Lord Provost *ex officio* and an assessor nominated by the Town Council. The infusion of municipal blood into the body academic at Edinburgh was intended as a compensation to the Town Council for their loss of control over the destinies of the University, but it was an experiment that was later imitated elsewhere with beneficial results to university administration. In section 19 of the act the universities were directed to exercise their powers in subordination to those of the executive commission, but on the expiration of the latter the initiative of altering or revoking any of their ordinances was vested, with certain safeguards, in each of the University Courts, so far as the particular ordinance related to that university. The commissioners in the exercise of their powers were in turn instructed to have special regard to the recommendations made by preceding Royal Commissions of inquiry. The main duties devolving upon them included revising foundations and altering trusts which had been in operation for 50 years or more, regulating the powers of university office-bearers and the election of officers such as the Chancellor and Rector, determining the requirements for university entrance and graduation, founding new chairs, providing for the administration of the university revenues and fixing the date on which various provisions of the act should come into operation.

The act contained a permissive clause proposing the foundation of a National University of Scotland, of which the existing institutions should become constituent colleges. A university on federal lines had already been tried out in Ireland and a similar scheme was later to be extended to Wales; the alleged advantage of such an arrangement was that by means of a central examining body a uniformly high standard of degrees would be obtained throughout the country. There can be no doubt that the previous laxity in this respect had been a subject of reproach to the Scottish universities, but it was inconceivable that such a scheme could be seriously considered. Nevertheless, the commissioners were instructed to inquire and report how far the proposal might be practicable and expedient. Since the consent of the Chancellor and University Court and the approval of the Senatus Academicus and General Council were required in each instance, it was hardly likely that any of the universities would agree to voluntary degradation to the rank of college. So the commissioners found after due inquiry and the proposal fell through.

The remaining provisions of the act dealt with the union of King's and Marischal Colleges to form the new University of Aberdeen and the application of the parliamentary grant to the Scottish universities. Under the first head the commissioners were instructed to determine the number of professors and classes that would be required in the united university, to abolish offices rendered unnecessary by the union, to arrange for compensation for those deprived of their offices in this way, to determine the right of patronage of the chairs created in the new university and to decide the uses to which the buildings of King's and Marischal Colleges should be put. Under the second head they were required to advise the Treasury on the allocation of the annual parliamentary grant, fixed for various purposes at £10,000 a year among the four universities. In addition to the compensation to displaced Aberdeen professors, the monies might be used for providing pensions for retired Principals and professors, for employing assistants to professors in office, for making payments to external examiners, for increasing existing salaries and for endowing new professorships where required.

In the discharge of their duties the commissioners drafted 90 ordinances, of which only one was disallowed. Some of these were general and applied equally to all the universities, others were applicable only to individual universities. Undoubtedly the commissioners' most important work related to the system of graduation, which they overhauled completely by establishing regulations for degrees in Arts, Law, and Medicine. In Divinity they were unable to reach agreement on account of the difficult situation created by the Disruption, but even there they left better equipped Divinity faculties at Glasgow and Aberdeen; they suggested that the universities themselves should introduce such regulations for graduation as they might see fit. They were confronted by certain difficulties in regard to graduation in Law and Medicine also, which they did their best to resolve. The University of St. Andrews, for instance, had no teaching in Law and very defective facilities in Medicine, while the Universities of Glasgow and Aberdeen could not provide all the courses required for graduation in Law. Only in Arts was complete uniformity possible.

The traditional curriculum for the degree of M.A. (or A.M., as it was then generally written) was a four years' course consisting of Latin, Greek, mathematics and the three medieval philosophies, metaphysical, moral and natural. The degree of B.A. had fallen into disuse in the three pre-Reformation universities and at Edinburgh had never been granted at all. At Glasgow it was revived in 1774 and occasionally granted after a three years' course of study which omitted mathematics and natural philosophy from the M.A. curriculum. It was thus merely an incomplete master's degree, and the recommendation of a first degree of B.A. which had been made by the Royal Commission of 1826-30 had the undesirable effect of stimulating other universities to imitate this rather questionable practice. Accordingly, St. Andrews and Edinburgh also instituted a B.A. degree, obtainable after three years' study, in 1839 and 1842 respectively. As Edinburgh had added a course in rhetoric to the requirements for the M.A. degree, the B.A. degree was less anomalous than elsewhere and omitted only the course in natural philosophy. On the other hand, the University of Edinburgh also conferred purely honorary M.A. degrees in many cases.

The commissioners very properly decided to abolish these anomalies. They suppressed the degree of B.A. altogether and ordained that in future the degree of M.A. should not be conferred *honoris causa tantum*. For the ordinary degree of M.A. they adopted the traditional curriculum plus the course in rhetoric (renamed English literature) that had latterly been required at Edinburgh. Following the recommendations of their predecessors they prescribed two years' attendance at the classes in Latin, Greek and Mathematics, and one year at those in logic and metaphysics, moral philosophy, natural philosophy and English literature. They did not introduce an entrance examination but allowed a year's remission in the case of students who on matriculation were fitted to pass an adequate preliminary test in the two classical languages. Thus by by-passing the junior classes in Latin and Greek promising students were encouraged to graduate in three instead of four years. The subjects of study in the Faculty of Arts were grouped for examination purposes under the heads of classical literature, mental philosophy (which included English literature), mathematics and natural philosophy, and natural science. Every candidate for the M.A. degree was required to satisfy the examiners in the first three, but the last, which included geology, zoology, chemistry and botany, was an innovation and merely permissive. Any university might, over and above the minimum requirement of attendance at the seven courses for the standard curriculum, prescribe attendance at one of the courses in the department of natural science as a necessary condition for graduation in Arts. Two of the universities actually did this, Aberdeen requiring attendance at the class of natural history, which included zoology and geology, and St. Andrews attendance at the class of chemistry.

Stimulated no doubt by the success of the Oxford honour schools and Cambridge triposes, the commissioners followed the recommendation of the Rosebery Commission by instituting graduation with honours. They ordained that any candidate, but only after satisfying the examiners in all the subjects prescribed for the ordinary degree, might take a further examination for honours in any one or more of the four departments, mental philosophy for this purpose including logic and metaphysics and moral philosophy but not English literature. Again on the recommendation of the previous commission, the commissioners introduced two classes of honours (although calling them simply first and second) in the departments of classical literature, mental philosophy and mathematics, but only one class in natural science. In this respect their regulations were not altogether satisfactory, for they made no provision for additional instruction in the case of honours candidates. This was particularly unfortunate as regards natural science, since no instruction in that department was necessarily required in the ordinary degree. Moreover, the courses provided in the universities were not always very adequate in any case. No botany was taught at all in St. Andrews and in the other universities geology was lumped together with zoology as part of the course in natural history. The inevitable result was that while few students graduated with honours in any department, scarcely any proceeded to honours in natural science.

In Medicine the commissioners replaced the traditional first degree of M.D. by a double degree in medicine and surgery, M.B., C.M. The degree of Master in Surgery was designed simply to give a specific qualification in that field, although it really added nothing to the single degree of M.B., for which the same examination was required. Thus candidates who had no need to prove their special training in the surgical field did not require to pay the additional fee, for which alone it was awarded, and could graduate without it. As a preliminary qualification the commissioners, guided once more by their predecessors, did not require graduation in Arts, but in default of it they prescribed the passing of a satisfactory examination in seven Arts subjects specified for the purpose. The professional course in Medicine was to extend over four academic years and, as previously for the M.D. degree, every candidate was required to submit a thesis. This left little scope for the M.D. degree, which, under the commissioners' regulations, might be conferred on M.B.s of not less than 24 years of age after two years' practical experience, provided that, if not already graduates in Arts, they had also passed a satisfactory examination in three Arts subjects conducted by the Faculty of Arts. Apart from the evidence of satisfactory professional experience, the M.D. degree did not therefore require any further medical knowledge, and so the University of Edinburgh soon began to agitate for a transfer of the thesis from the first stage to the second, to maintain a better proportion between the two.

In Law the commissioners left the traditional degree of LL.D. honorary as before but introduced a new degree of LL.B. which could be taken by examination. It was limited to graduates in Arts and entailed a three years' course of study of a more comprehensive nature than that prescribed by the 1826-30 commission. In addition to the courses in civil law, Scots law, and conveyancing the commissioners required attendance at courses in public law, constitutional law and history, and medical jurisprudence. In Divinity they saw that each university was provided with four theological chairs in divinity, Biblical criticism, ecclesiastical history and Hebrew. The degree of D.D. continued to be awarded as an honorary distinction although one or two of the universities occasionally awarded it by thesis, but in 1864, shortly after the expiration of the commissioners' powers, the individual universities took the initiative and instituted the degree of B.D., obtainable by graduates in Arts after a systematic course of study in the four departments of theology.

The work of the commissioners thus left the universities constitutionally autonomous, administratively reorganized, and equipped with a system of graduation in all four faculties. Subsequent experience showed that in Arts their requirements for graduation were unnecessarily procrustean and this had important repercussions on graduation in Science and Law. Undoubtedly they ought to have accorded a more prominent place to Science in their scheme of studies, for the meagre recognition they gave did very little to bring science teaching within the graduation system. For ordinary graduation the two larger universities failed to include any department of natural science as a compulsory course, and every candidate for honours in natural science was compelled to go through the whole linguistic and philosophic section of the curriculum in all the universities. This was hardly conducive to specialization in an increasingly important branch of study. In England, on the other hand, the University of Cambridge introduced a special natural science tripos in 1851, Oxford an honours school of natural science in 1853, and London a Faculty of Science with the degrees of B.Sc. and D.Sc. in 1860. The consequence was that in 1864 the University of Edinburgh short-circuited the commissioners' elaborate arrangements by establishing the new degrees of B.Sc. and D.Sc., on the London model, within the Faculty of Arts. The degree of B.Sc. was awarded in the four departments of mathematical, physical and natural science, and engineering, to which public health was later added. The degree of D.Sc. was likewise conferred in these departments on the submission of a thesis, and also, somewhat anomalously, in mental science or philology.

In Law, there was the double inconvenience of the necessity of previous graduation in Arts and the fact that candidates for the full LL.B. course were compelled to go to the University of Edinburgh to complete their degree. Accordingly, in 1874 the two universities of Glasgow and Edinburgh took concerted action to introduce a new degree in law in addition to the existing LL.B. The B.L. degree was to be a first degree, including some Arts subjects and fewer law courses than were required for the full law degree. Consequently, candidates who were not already graduates in Arts had to pass a preliminary examination in four Arts subjects, attend one course of lectures in the Faculty of Arts, and take four of the six prescribed courses in law. Of these civil law, Scots law and conveyancing were compulsory, but the candidate was allowed to choose any one of the other three at his option.

In 1868 the privilege of returning members to Parliament, granted to Oxford and Cambridge (before the Union of the Parliaments) by James I in 1603, was extended to the four Scottish universities by the Representation of the People (Scotland) Act. For this purpose the universities were grouped into two constituencies, Edinburgh with St. Andrews, and Glasgow with Aberdeen, each returning one member; the franchise was based on membership of the General Council. By the same act the General Councils were enlarged to include, in addition to the M.A.s and M.D.s, those who had proceeded to any of the newer degrees, such as B.D. or B.Sc., or indeed 'any other degree that may hereafter be instituted', and at the same time the requirement of four years' attendance at classes in the university granting the degree was dropped.

The enfranchisement of the universities was tangible proof of the increased prestige resulting from the reforms effected under the act of 1858, but experience indicated the desirability of still further reform. This opinion was encouraged by the appointment of a Royal Commission for Oxford and Cambridge, to review the workings of the acts of 1854 and 1856, under the chairmanship of the Duke of Cleveland. This commission was appointed in 1872 and its report led to the Oxford and Cambridge Universities Act of 1877, by which a permanent Universities Committee of the Privy Council was constituted to deal with their affairs. In April 1876 another Royal Commission was appointed to inquire into various matters connected with the universities of Scotland, presided over by John Inglis, former chairman of the executive commission of 1858-62. Among the other eleven members were such distinguished names as those of Lord Playfair, J. A. Froude and T. H. Huxley. The commission's terms of reference included inquiry into the constitutions of the various University Courts, the functions of the General Councils, the regulations for graduation, the expediency of establishing new faculties or degrees, the financial position of the universities and the condition of their buildings. It sat for two years and in 1878 issued a comprehensive report containing minutes of evidence from 112 witnesses and 61 recommendations made by the commissioners themselves.

The commissioners proposed to enlarge the numbers of the University Courts to include three (instead of one) representatives of the General Council and two (instead of one) representatives of the Senatus Academicus. At St. Andrews, however, it was suggested that the second Principal should be an *ex officio* member in lieu of the additional assessor from the Senatus Academicus. In the matter of alterations to existing ordinances the commissioners recommended a more standardized procedure: so long as the machinery instituted by the act of 1858 remained in force, they felt that any University Court, before applying to the Privy Council for permission to make a change, should be obliged to intimate the proposed alteration to the other three Courts. Even this, however, was not considered entirely satisfactory, and the commissioners proposed the establishment of some supervisory body. A standing committee of the Privy Council they did not regard as practicable in the case of the Scottish universities and recommended instead a 'General Universities Court for Scotland'. This body, comprising the four Chancellors, a representative chosen by the Senatus Academicus of each university, and three nominees of the Crown, was to serve as a general Court of Appeal from individual University Courts, to sanction new ordinances and changes in existing ones, and to report to the Crown on any university matters that might be referred to it. The only suggestion for improvement in the constitution of the General Councils that the commissioners had to make was that in each university rectors, principals and professors should be deemed members for life, if not otherwise so qualified, and not merely so long as they happened to hold office.

Under the head of graduation the commissioners had several important recommendations to put forward. In Arts they suggested that while the uniform curriculum laid down by the executive commission had great cultural value, it often bore little relation to the prospective careers of many of the students. To ensure the continuance of a broad general basis they proposed that before embarking on a course for graduation all candidates should be required to pass a 'first examination' in Latin, Greek, mathematics and English, and preferably also in elementary physical and natural science when the facilities for this were available. The first examination might be taken either directly from school or prepared for within the university itself, but attendance for this purpose would not count for graduation. The course of graduation proper would then extend over three academic years and consist either of the subjects already in force or alternatively of specialization along one of five lines. *Literature and Philology* would comprise classics, English and one other language; *Philosophy* would include logic and metaphysics, ethics, psychology and physiology; *Law and History* would comprise civil law, constitutional or international law, political economy and a branch of ancient or modern history; *Mathematical Science* would include pure and applied mathematics, natural philosophy and astronomy; and *Natural Science* would comprise natural philosophy and chemistry, with a selection from applied mathematics, physiology, botany, zoology and geology.

The commissioners rejected any proposal for reviving the B.A. degree, and recommended that no special examination should be set for honours. In their view, the requirements for honours should simply be greater proficiency in the same subjects, shown in the ordinary examination, and only one class of honours ought to be awarded. For graduation in Law, Medicine and Science the commissioners proposed to institute a first examination similar to that in Arts, except that candidates for other degrees might elect to take a translation test from French and German in place of the systematic examination in Greek required for graduation in Arts.

They found that degrees in Science had been instituted at Glasgow and St. Andrews as well as at Edinburgh and, while commending the innovation, they were not prepared to advocate a separate Faculty of Science. They recommended, however, that the requirements for the B.Sc. degree should be so far as possible assimilated in the different universities, and even indicated, though not very precisely, their own conceptions of suitable options for the course. These would consist of certain combinations of the courses prescribed for the specialized M.A. degree in the mathematical and natural science groups, but would apparently demand rather more than was required for graduation in Arts. In Medicine the commissioners advocated that candidates, having passed the same first examination as for Science, should also be examined at a later stage in the purely scientific parts of their professional course, so as to leave only the practical subjects of medicine and surgery for their final examination. They very properly recommended that every candidate should graduate with the double degree of M.B., Ch.B., and that the mastership in surgery should be reserved as an extra distinction for specialists in the surgical field. They had no special recommendations to make in regard to graduation in Law or Divinity, but they suggested that, in view of the Reid chair of music at Edinburgh, that university might confer honorary degrees in music though not degrees by examination.

As regards new professorships, they strongly urged the foundation of chairs in history and in geology, and recommended the institution of lectureships in French and German. Like their predecessors of 50 years earlier, they drew attention to the propriety of instituting some check on the foundation of new chairs and proposed that the sanction of the General Universities Court should be required for that purpose. At Edinburgh they recommended that the number of curators of patronage should be increased by two to include a representative of the General Council and the President for the time being of the Royal Society of Edinburgh. They proposed that the patronage of three chairs at St. Andrews should be transferred from individual noblemen to the University Court or the Crown. In all the universities the right of appointment to lectureships should be vested in the Senatus

Academicus. They recommended that the minimum salary of a full-time professor should be £600 per annum and proposed that the Principals at Edinburgh and Glasgow should receive £1200 a year, the Principal at Aberdeen £800 and the Senior Principal at St. Andrews £700. They considered it preferable, however, that the two St. Andrews colleges should be united into one corporate body, to be called the University of St. Andrews, of which only one Principal would be the ordinary head.

Without making any specific recommendation the commissioners examined the possibility of combining the educational resources of Dundee with those of St. Andrews. They considered four suggested expedients: firstly, the transfer of the seat of the University to Dundee; secondly, the enlargement of the University at St. Andrews by the addition of new chairs in science and medicine; thirdly, the establishment of a complete college in Dundee *pari passu* with those in St. Andrews; fourthly, the founding of a complementary college in Dundee, affiliated to a unified University of St. Andrews and offering instruction in the mathematical, physical and natural sciences, and in Medicine. They themselves expressed a slight preference for the last of these alternatives.

No immediate action was taken, however, on their report as a whole. The commissioners estimated that while some of their recommendations could be effected by the universities themselves and a number might be enacted by a change of ordinance, twenty-four would require legislation and nine would involve parliamentary votes of money. A bill based on the report of the Inglis Commission was introduced as early as 1883 but it was not until six years later that legislation, after several attempts, was at last secured. An act for the better administration and endowment of the universities of Scotland was finally passed on 30th August 1889 and became effective on 1st January 1890. This measure amplified the provisions of the act of 1858 and still largely governs the workings of the Scottish universities at the present day.

In the meantime, local action in Dundee had gone ahead with plans for developing university education in the city independently of any formal connection with St. Andrews. In 1881 a University College, on the model of those established during the nineteenth century in the larger English provincial towns, was projected; it was opened in 1883. It comprised two Arts chairs (classics and English) and eight science chairs (mathematics, physics, chemistry, engineering, botany, natural history, anatomy and physiology), and, like its English counterparts, it at first prepared students for external degrees of the University of London. In 1885, however, in view of the predominantly scientific nature of the instruction provided, an agreement was reached with the University of St. Andrews by which the St. Andrews science degree was made available instead of the London one. But there was no other link between the two institutions.

PART IV

THE LATTER PART OF THE CENTURY

CHAPTER VII

ELEMENTARY EDUCATION 1873-1903

FOR their investigation into the working of the specific subjects in state-aided schools, to which domestic economy had been added as a compulsory subject for girls in the code of 1876, the Moncrieff commissioners decided to issue a separate report in terms of the eleventh section of the Endowed Institutions (Scotland) Act of 1878. They examined fourteen expert witnesses on the question and their report appeared in 1881. Contrary to expectations, their findings were on the whole not unfavourable to the system of specific subjects, although they strongly criticized the value of the science subjects as they were then taught. They suggested certain improvements on the existing system, from which, however, little resulted.

Among their recommendations was a proposal to raise the standard of the teacher in training by requiring prospective pupil teachers to have attained the third stage in at least two of the specific subjects before allowing them to enter on their engagements. They further recommended a widening of the basis of their subsequent education during training and proposed that scholarships and allowances should be continued for a third session to encourage the attendance of teachers at the university. In the second place, the commissioners, while unable to advocate a secondary school within reach of all, recommended that in every parish there should be at least one teacher qualified to give instruction in the higher subjects. Thirdly, they considered that in schools where the average attendance exceeded 140 pupils the minimum staffing ratio required by the code should be increased. Fourthly, they suggested that the number of specific subjects should be reduced from fourteen to nine by dropping the science subjects except for physical geography and animal physiology. Fifthly, they agreed with the contention that a larger grant should be made for a pass in a higher stage of a subject than for one at a lower stage, although they were unwilling to adjudicate between the educative value of the different subjects themselves. Sixthly, they recommended that elementary science should be taught by object lessons only, and that a special allowance for the efficient teaching of such subjects should be made in the administration of the parliamentary grant. Finally, to encourage the teaching of higher subjects in thinly populated districts, the commissioners urged a relaxation in the strictness of the regulations for payment of grants, to allow of their being paid on the general proficiency of a class instead of the number of pupils in attendance. The Department paid small heed to these proposals, but the code of 1883 recognized agriculture as a specific subject and Gaelic was added to the list in 1884.

The decade of the eighties was one of considerable activity in educational matters. In August 1883 an education act was passed to tighten up attendance at school and to bring the provisions of factory and educational legislation into harmony with one another. In England Lord Sandon's Act of 1876 had raised the school-leaving age from thirteen to fourteen, unless attendance or proficiency exempted a child at an earlier age, and by the Factory and Workshop Act of 1878 full-time employment was limited to children over fourteen, except for those who had gained exemption at thirteen. The Education (Scotland) Act of 1883, accordingly, likewise raised the leaving age from thirteen to fourteen and restricted exemption to proficiency only, fixed by section 7 as the fifth standard. The act thus brought into alignment the age up to which a child could be compelled to attend school and that up to which he could be prevented from going into full-time employment. Half-time employment was, however, still permitted between ten and fourteen, provided the child had passed the third standard and continued with such part-time education as was prescribed by the minutes of the Department. Finally, to enable school boards to take more direct and effectual proceedings against negligent parents, the machinery of 'attendance orders' was extended to Scotland. This had also been introduced in England by Lord Sandon's Act, and it enabled a board, after due warning to a recalcitrant parent, to complain to a court of summary jurisdiction and have an order made out naming a school which the child should attend. The superiority of this measure lay in the fact that any infringement of the order was easily and quickly proved. The act further empowered the Department to effect the compulsory combination of two or more school boards to meet cases of educational deficiency, such action having previously been at the discretion of the boards themselves subject to the sanction of the Department.

A much more thoroughgoing reform was the complete separation of the Scotch from the English Education Department in 1885. By the Secretary for Scotland Act of that year the Vice-President of the Committee of Council on Education was replaced as vice-president of the Scottish committee by the Secretary for Scotland, whose office was revived by the statute after a lapse of a century and a half. The Lord President of the Council remained nominally president of both committees *ex officio*, but the Scottish Secretary now became the responsible parliamentary minister in respect of educational matters relating to Scotland, and the Department's autonomy was greatly enhanced by the appointment of a separate permanent secretary. The new office was given to Mr. (later Sir) Henry Craik, and the authority of Mr. Patrick Cumin, who had succeeded Sir Francis Sandford in the previous year, was henceforth limited to England and Wales.

Although the headquarters of the Scotch Education Department remained in London at Dover House, Whitehall, the reorganization heralded important modifications in Scottish education. The Code of 1886, for instance, abolished individual examination in the first two standards of the primary school and substituted graduated grants, based on H.M. Inspector's report, instead. The code also enriched the primary school curriculum by introducing 'class' subjects, in place of specific subjects, below the fifth standard. Such subjects included English language and literature, geography, history, elementary science, drawing and needlework, and had been in force in the English code since 1875. For this purpose, therefore, the first three were removed from the category of specific subjects, which were now restricted to standards five and six, and ex-standard pupils, for the award of grants. Finally, the new code further adopted the recommendation of the Moncrieff commission regarding the payment of grants for the teaching of higher subjects in sparsely populated districts by increasing the grant from 4/- to 10/-, in seven highland and island counties, for the more difficult specific subjects such as mathematics and Latin.

Towards the close of the same year (1886) the Secretary for Scotland also set up a departmental committee, under the chairmanship of the veteran C.S. Parker, M.P., to inquire into certain questions relating to education in Scotland. The committee sat for two years and issued three reports covering practically the whole field of Scottish education, apart from the universities, although the order in which they presented their findings was somewhat haphazard. The first report appeared in February 1887 and recommended changes in the Scotch code to facilitate the admission of Gaelic-speaking students as

Queen's Scholars to training colleges, with a view to providing a supply of trained Gaelic-speaking teachers for the highlands. This was given effect to in the code of 1887, which enabled pupil teachers from highland counties to take a paper set in Gaelic in the examination for entrance to the colleges.

The second report, which appeared in 1888, dealt with the training colleges themselves and set forth the committee's views on the whole question of teacher training. The members recognized that the professional training of teachers should be given mainly in specially organized institutions, but they also believed that it should be combined where possible with the liberalizing influence of university education. At the same time, however, they concluded that the general education should also be undertaken by these institutions, except in the case of students who were able to profit from higher education at a university or even a technical college. In the case of such students they recommended that during the university session the training college curriculum should be revised to leave the time mainly free for the requirements of university classes. They found also that the professional training of university students should be concentrated into a shorter time and proposed that graduates should be recognized as qualified teachers after a six months' course in a practising school. To encourage the principle of training, as opposed to mere certification after examination, they recommended that college or university trained teachers should be regarded as qualified to teach a larger number of pupils than other certificated teachers. On the question of denominational control they advocated that the existing system of grants to the Church of Scotland and Free Church colleges be continued, with the proviso that a share in the work should be assigned on the same terms to any other body equally well qualified and willing to undertake the financial responsibility. As regards cost they concluded that it was moderate and should neither be reduced nor charged more heavily to the students in training, but they found the existing payment of grants, based upon three-quarters of the actual expenditure incurred, unnecessarily complicated.

The committee's third report, issued also in 1888, treated of the rather unrelated topics of secondary education and compulsory attendance. Its recommendations under the first head will be discussed elsewhere, and under the second it had little to contribute. In general the committee considered that the existing powers of compulsion, if rigorously applied, should suffice, but in the special case of country districts the Department should use vigilance in accepting ordinary rural occupations as a 'reasonable excuse' for non-attendance at school. To meet the case of neglected children in large towns, they also recommended that the power of establishing 'day industrial schools' should be given, as in England by the act of 1876 or in the isolated instance of Glasgow by a local act of 1878.

An important development in administration was the creation of County Councils as a result of the Local Government (Scotland) Act of 1889 following upon a similar measure for England and Wales passed in the previous year. This measure was to have two significant, if indirect, effects upon the Scottish educational tradition: firstly, the gradual supersession of the parish as the unit of local organization, and, secondly, the abandonment of the immemorial custom of charging fees in Scottish schools. The second of these changes was, however, more rapidly effected than the first. Under the English act the new local authorities had been granted an income out of probate and licence duties to be devoted to certain specific purposes; the balance was to be utilized for the relief of local taxation. Under the Scottish measure an amount equal to eleven-hundredths of this sum was authorized for similar purposes, but at the request of the Scottish M.P.s the balance, amounting to nearly a quarter of a million sterling, was assigned to the relief of school fees in grant-aided schools and not to the aid of local taxation. The disposal of this sum was left to the discretion of the Department, which by a minute of August 1889 decreed the remission of all fees below the fourth standard and partial remission in the fourth and fifth standards.

The policy of freeing elementary education created a precedent in Great Britain as a whole, and so far as Scotland was concerned was continued in the following year as a result of the Local Taxation (Customs and Excise) Act of 1890. This act, applicable to all parts of Great Britain, disposed of a large sum of money raised to compensate publicans for loss of licence in a drive to reduce the number of public-houses throughout the country, an object which, however, failed to command the approval of Parliament. Instead, the money was assigned to police superannuation and the residue voted to the further relief of local taxation by distribution among local authorities, with the option (on the motion of Mr. A. H. D. Acland) of using the whole or any part of it to assist technical education. The grant, accordingly, came to be known as the 'Residue Grant' and on account of its source it was often popularly referred to as the 'Whisky Money'. As a first charge on the Scottish share, however, a sum not exceeding £40,000 was set aside for additional relief of school fees and by this means the Department in a minute of August 1890 was enabled to free standards four and five entirely.

Then in June 1891 fees for all children between 5 and 14, without reference to standard, were remitted. This did not prevent the school boards from retaining at their discretion a small number of fee-paying schools, provided they satisfied the Department that they had already made adequate provision for free education in their district. Meanwhile, England began to follow suit and the Elementary Education Act of 1891 granted the sum of 10/- a year for each child between 3 and 15 in average attendance at public elementary schools, on condition that fees were abolished except where they had previously exceeded that amount. As Scotland had voluntarily sacrificed relief of local taxation for this purpose, equity demanded a revision of section 22 of the Local Government Act of 1889. Accordingly, the Education and Local Taxation Account (Scotland) Act of 1892 made over to Scotland an 'Equivalent Grant' of £265,000 for the relief of school fees and set free the money previously assigned for it, but stipulated that out of the latter £60,000 should be made available for secondary education and £30,000 for the universities. Finally, in 1893, education was made free for all pupils between 3 and 15, as it had been in England since 1891.

Meanwhile the code of 1890 abolished individual examination as the basis of payment for grants in the three elementary subjects throughout the school, and proposed instead a fixed grant of 10/- per pupil in average attendance, plus a graduated payment up to 3/- (or 3/6 above the third standard) for merit in teaching. At the same time the system of specific subjects was considerably modified and the number reduced to seven: mathematics, Latin, Greek, French, German, agriculture and domestic economy. The object of this was to simplify the curriculum, but an opportunity was afforded to managers of state-aided schools to adapt their scheme of work to local conditions by allowing them to select additional subjects at their discretion. They had, however, to submit a graduated scheme to be approved by the Department, and any scientific subjects chosen were required to be taught principally by experiment and illustration.

A further attempt to introduce some unity into the primary school curriculum was made in the code of 1892, which instituted the Merit Certificate. This certificate experienced several vicissitudes before being finally stabilized, but in the first instance it was intended as a kind of leaving certificate awarded at the end of the compulsory period of schooling. Therefore, it was open to pupils of over 13 in state-aided elementary schools who satisfied H.M. Inspector in the three elementary subjects, at least two class subjects and all three stages of one specific subject. It offered a definite goal at which to aim, and the response to this innovation was highly satisfactory. In the same year the Leaving Certificate, instituted in 1888 for the benefit of higher class (or secondary) schools, was made available to suitable candidates from state-aided elementary schools.

In view of the financial difficulties involved in extending higher class schools, many school boards had organized higher departments in elementary schools by means of the specific subjects, supplementing the grants for these by satisfying the requirements of the Science and Art Department as well as by payments out of the school fund. They were thus able to keep the fees more moderate than the majority of secondary schools proper, and in a very few years they presented more than twice as many candidates for the Leaving Certificate as the higher class schools themselves. As yet, however, there was no satisfactory criterion for determining the completion of an adequate primary education before the pupil embarked upon a post-primary course, either in a higher class school or a higher department of an elementary school. Consequently in 1898 the function of the Merit Certificate was changed and it was henceforth recognized as the dividing line between the two. As the Department worked out the age of the break at about 12, the age qualification of the Merit Certificate was lowered to 12 and the requirement regarding proficiency in a specific subject was dispensed with.

The first thoroughgoing attempt to co-ordinate the post-primary curriculum in elementary schools was made in the code of 1899, by which the specific subjects were at length finally superseded. In general their place was taken by Advanced Departments, in which the curriculum was to be specifically approved for each school by the Department, admission being made conditional on possession of the Merit Certificate. The size of class was restricted to not more than 40 pupils and a grant of 50/- per annum, based on average attendance, was to be made. The Department prescribed a basic curriculum of English, geography, history, arithmetic and drawing at the senior stage, and recommended that additional subjects in languages, mathematics and experimental science should also be included for approval in any syllabus submitted. At the junior stage greater liberty was likewise given to managers in the curriculum offered, only nature knowledge and drawing being made compulsory apart from the three elementary subjects. The new Advanced Departments were primarily intended for pupils likely to leave school at the end of the compulsory period of education, which terminated at fourteen in the ordinary case or at thirteen if exemption had been secured by examination or granted by the school board for compassionate reasons. The attendance of the average pupil in an Advanced Department was thus unlikely to exceed two years, a fact which necessarily limited the possible scope of the curriculum.

To meet the needs of such pupils as were likely to remain at school for a longer period with a view to taking up industrial or commercial occupations, another and more ambitious type of reorganization was also sanctioned by the same code. This was the Higher Grade Department or School, which was more definitely secondary in character. At first vocational in bias, such schools were required to provide a well-defined course of instruction extending over not less than three years. Classes were limited to a maximum of thirty pupils and grants were made on the scale of 50/- per annum in the first year (as in the case of Advanced Departments) but rising by an additional 20/- in each subsequent year and allowing also for a special increment for exceptional efficiency. The basic curriculum was once more English, geography, history, higher arithmetic and drawing, but it had to include also either mathematics, experimental science and manual work, or else one or more modern languages, book-keeping and shorthand, according to which of the two recognized categories the particular school was in. These were in the one case Higher Grade Science Departments, predominantly scientific and technical, and in the other Higher Grade Commercial Departments.

To give point and direction to the curriculum, an Intermediate Certificate was introduced in 1902, which might be taken by candidates of not less than 15 years of age who had passed in four or more subjects in the Leaving Certificate examination, including one at least on the higher standard. This was intended as a leaving certificate for those who could not remain long enough at school to take the full Leaving Certificate, and though it was awarded from the beginning as a 'group' certificate, individual subjects might at first be attempted by younger candidates and were credited towards the certificate. But, like its counterpart at the junior stage, the Merit Certificate, the Intermediate Certificate tended to change its function from time to time.

Meanwhile, however, the Elementary Education Act of 1900 empowered English school boards to make by-laws raising the age of compulsory attendance from 13 to 14 without exemption, and at the same time tightened up the minimal conditions of exemption where advantage was not taken of this provision. This was not greatly in advance of the existing position in Scotland since 1883, where in any case exemption had been more strictly regulated. Nevertheless, it was followed in 1901 by an Education (Scotland) Act which limited still further the powers of school boards in the matter and abolished exemption by examination at 13, thus virtually raising the leaving age to 14 throughout the country. The act was operative from 1st January 1902, and although the original phraseology of the statute of 1872, namely '(efficient) elementary education in reading, writing, and arithmetic', was retained, the Department undertook further reorganization of post-primary courses to meet the new situation. The Merit Certificate was once again put back to mark the successful completion of an advanced curriculum, and its place as a determinant of readiness for such a curriculum was taken by the 'qualifying examination' in 1903. The latter was a written test, conferring no certificate and originally conducted by the Department through H.M. Inspectors.

In the same year the Advanced Departments, though they had been in operation for only four years, were replaced by what were to be called 'Supplementary Courses' with a vocational bias. They were open to children over 12 who had passed the qualifying examination, and the conditions as to grant and size of classes remained unaltered. The aim of these courses was stated to be not only to continue the studies of the primary school but to emphasize their meaning in relation to future occupations, to produce good citizens and to prepare the pupils for the rational enjoyment of leisure. To this end the somewhat general character of the Advanced Departments was modified in favour of a curriculum which was partly general, including English, health education and social history, and partly vocational in nature. Under this latter head a choice of four special courses was given, either commercial, industrial, rural, or household management, and the Merit Certificate might be awarded to pupils who had satisfactorily pursued one of them for not less than a year.

Many well-meaning educationists deplored the new policy of early specialization, and the Supplementary Courses were criticized almost as severely as the former specific subjects, but, like them, they survived all opposition for a matter of twenty years. In the interests of efficiency a certain amount of centralization was introduced in many places, particularly in the larger burghs, and such courses were conducted at separate central schools, to which several neighbouring primary schools sent those pupils who had succeeded in passing the qualifying examination. By a curious *volte-face* in the official viewpoint, the Higher Grade Departments, on the other hand, were liberalized and the former element of specialization abolished. Again no change was made in the system of grants or pupil-teacher ratio, but the curriculum was broadened and now directed specifically to preparing pupils for the newly instituted Intermediate Certificate. The basic curriculum had to include English, geography and history, mathematics and arithmetic, one foreign language, science and drawing.

At the same time, the larger and better organized Advanced Departments were permitted to become Higher Grade Schools in their reformed guise. Under the new regulations, therefore, the latter were no longer either science or commercial departments but virtually secondary schools, though administered under the Scotch code like other elementary schools. Indeed, they and the former Advanced Departments (now Supplementary Courses) had almost exactly reversed their previous roles as regards the nature of the education they supplied. The new tendency for the Higher Grade Schools to approximate to the earlier years of the secondary school proper was further emphasized by a change in the function of the Intermediate Certificate three years later. In 1906, in addition to testifying to the successful completion of an intermediate course of general education, its possession was made compulsory on all candidates for the Leaving Certificate proper. Consequently, it ceased to be awarded on an isolated subject basis on the papers set for the latter, and became a curriculum certificate, oral and written, specially based on the approved subjects of each particular school and taken at one examination.

The special importance of the new Higher Grade Schools lies in the fact that they once again connected the former parish schools with the universities, thereby perpetuating the Scottish educational tradition, for many of them carried their abler pupils right up to the Leaving Certificate. They never received explicit statutory recognition as such, but the expression 'intermediate school', first employed by the Department in 1906 and later incorporated in the interpretative section of the act of 1908, was generally equated with the term 'higher grade school'. In any case, they rapidly increased in number, and by 1910 there were nearly two hundred of them as against a more or less static fifty-five higher class public schools. In 1911 their status was further enhanced by a requirement of the Department that in each department of study there should be at least one teacher qualified under Chapter V of the regulations for the training of teachers. Then, in June 1920, five-year Higher Grade Schools were eventually fully recognized as secondary schools by the Department, the only important points of difference being that they generally charged no fees since they were eligible for grants under the code, and that the education they provided was on 'modern' rather than 'classical' lines. After the reorganization of the Intermediate Certificate in 1906 a limited degree of specialization was reintroduced into these schools at the post-certificate stage. Thus, those of them which went beyond the minimum three years' course might, during the last two years, provide literary courses leading to the Leaving Certificate, technical or commercial courses with a vocational bias, or courses in domestic economy specially suited to girls.

CHAPTER VIII

SECONDARY EDUCATION 1878-1908

IN THE reform of endowments, which was so vital to the development of the financially starved system of secondary education in Scotland, the Moncrieff Commission, through no fault of its own, achieved comparatively little. The commissioners issued two annual reports in which they stated that they had received thirty-two petitions for alterations in the government and administration of endowed institutions. The total annual revenue involved amounted to some £38,340, and in twenty-eight cases they were able to recommend to the Department that the powers asked for should, subject to certain modifications, be granted. But the annual revenue of the institutions in question amounted to a mere £16,652, less than half the total, and the only important endowment included was Robert Gordon's Hospital, Aberdeen. In 1881 this latter foundation was granted a provisional order permitting it to become a day school with the title of Robert Gordon's College. In the four remaining cases, in which the aggregate annual revenue was £21,688, the commissioners were constrained to recommend that the provisional orders applied for should be refused, and among the institutions that were unsuccessful were the governing bodies of George Heriot's Hospital and the Madras College, St. Andrews.

It was a meagre result for three years' labour, and to remedy the lack of initiative which had handicapped the commission in the execution of its task, a fresh measure was passed by Parliament on 18th August 1882. This was the Educational Endowments (Scotland) Act, intended to reorganize completely all endowments made before the passing of the education act of 1872, and extensive powers were given to a body of commissioners not only to inquire into the management of such endowments but to draw up schemes for their better administration in future. For this purpose the Queen was authorized, in section 4 of the act, to appoint seven commissioners once more to carry out the provisions of the statute, with powers of making and approving schemes up to 31st December 1887. The commission was duly appointed under the chairmanship of Lord Balfour of Burleigh on 26th August 1882 and the act came into force on 1st November of that year, but it eventually proved necessary to continue the commissioners' powers for two years beyond the original date. The commission thus remained in existence for over seven years and on 31st December of each year it issued its annual report. These consisted chiefly of the oral evidence taken from witnesses in connection with individual endowments investigated, but the volumes testify to the extraordinary care and thoroughness with which the commissioners performed the duties entrusted to them. Indeed, they completely overhauled the whole system of educational endowments in Scotland and as a result of their labours no further review was considered necessary for forty years. In general, the procedure adopted by the commissioners was to call before them the governing bodies of endowments of £50 annual value and upwards, and to employ the services of an assistant commissioner to inquire into smaller endowments.

The main objects which the commissioners were instructed to keep in view in dealing with these endowments were to extend their usefulness, to carry out more fully the spirit of the founder's intentions, having regard to the altered circumstances of the time, and so far as possible to set aside an adequate portion to enable boys and girls of promise to obtain higher education of the kind best suited to aid their advancement in life. In section 7 they were specifically directed to pay particular attention to making provision for secondary or technical education, in public schools or otherwise, in the districts to which the endowments belonged. The commissioners naturally interpreted these instructions as implying the development of higher education in the country as a whole, but they were careful not to divert too great a proportion of endowments from their primary purpose of subsidizing elementary education.

Despite the provisions of the act of 1872 and the machinery for obtaining gratuitous education, they were satisfied that a considerable sum might be judiciously expended on the relief of school fees during the compulsory period of schooling. Above the fifth standard, when compulsion ceased to operate, they were constrained to provide, in addition, school bursaries to be awarded by competition to children who were free to leave school, as a means of inducing them to remain on for a year or two after the compulsory period. Quite properly they did not regard such bursaries as leading necessarily to higher education or professional life but simply as intended to give such children an opportunity of obtaining a better education before passing into whatever trade or occupation they would naturally have chosen in any case. They did, however, endeavour to promote higher education in the strict sense by instituting special bursaries to be held at secondary schools and technical institutions for a period of two or three years, and they issued schemes for reforming all the outstanding hospitals and other establishments, such as Heriot's Hospital, Edinburgh; the Morgan Hospital, Dundee; and the Madras College, St. Andrews.

Some idea of the extent of the work achieved by the commission may be gathered from the fact that it submitted to the Department, 379 schemes dealing with 821 endowments (many smaller endowments in the same locality being combined in the interests of greater efficiency). The total annual revenue thus disposed of the commissioners estimated in the region of £200,000. Secondary education benefited substantially from it in the form of direct assistance to higher class schools and technical institutions, bursaries for such schools and universities, grants to school boards for establishing a system of higher education and school bursaries for pupils who had passed the fifth standard. The annual income devoted to these purposes was respectively £32,189 (higher class schools) and £22,200 (technical institutions), £21,954 (bursaries), £13,176 (grants to school boards) and £13,386 (school bursaries), making a grand total of approximately £103,000 per annum.

Of the remaining revenue an interesting item was the allocation of £14,259 for the education of girls, in addition to what they shared with boys. Under section 17 of the act the commissioners had been instructed to extend to both sexes, so far as could be equitably arranged, the benefit of endowments when framing schemes. This was in line with a recommendation of the Colebrooke Commission, and the commissioners themselves expressed sympathy for such an object. The education of women has, admittedly, except at the university level, not played anything like so great a part in the history of Scottish education as did the nineteenth century movement in favour of it in the development of education in England. In the sphere of girls' secondary education there are no names to compare with those of Miss Buss of the North London Collegiate School, or Miss Beale of Cheltenham Ladies' College; nor was there such extensive activity in the founding of trusts, such as the Girls' Public Day School Company in 1872 or the Church Schools Company eleven years later. This is no doubt to be accounted for by the co-educational nature of the instruction provided in the parish and many of the smaller burgh schools.

In some of the larger cities, however, where the need was felt to exist, the movement had some influence and led to the establishment of separate girls' schools. Of these perhaps the most celebrated was St. Leonard's School, St. Andrews, founded in 1877 on the site of the former St. Leonard's College of the University. In Edinburgh St. George's School was established in 1888, and in Glasgow the Girls' School Company, founded in 1879 and modelled on its English predecessor, was responsible for establishing the Park School in 1880 and similar schools at Helensburgh in 1895 and Kilmacolm in 1897. The residual revenue from endowments amounted to some £82,000 and was assigned by the commissioners to such purposes as free education, clothing and maintenance, evening classes and miscellaneous educational purposes. Under the first of these heads their efforts were to some extent negatived by the Local Government (Scotland) Act of 1889, in consequence of which fees for education in the early standards were largely abolished; but section 85 of the same act provided that any funds set free in this way should be disposed of by the governing bodies concerned after approval from the Department.

The Balfour of Burleigh Commission, notwithstanding the undoubted services which it had rendered to Scottish education, regretted the limitations under which the work had necessarily been carried on, perhaps the chief of which had been the inability to redistribute endowments according to density of population or other considerations. For this reason they were not in a position to claim to have established a complete and satisfactory system of higher education for Scotland as a whole, since educational facilities throughout the country were determined rather as opportunity offered than by any consistent plan. They therefore observed that the full benefit of their reforms could not be enjoyed until some order was introduced into the system of higher education which the endowments were designed to foster.

Meanwhile, two potential developments were taking place during the life-time of the commission. The first of these was the well-intentioned Technical Schools (Scotland) Act of 1887, by which school boards were permitted to establish a school, or department of a school, in which technical instruction should be given. By a strange paradox this was the first measure passed by Parliament for technical education in Great Britain, for Scotland was not a highly industrialized country and her educational tradition had been predominantly academic, with the result that hardly any use was made of it. The provisions of the act were somewhat complicated but the main powers it conferred were as follows. After the spring elections of 1888 a school board might pass a resolution to provide a technical school for its district. Such a school would rank as a secondary school in so far as it would come under section 18 of the act of 1878, which defined the powers of school boards as regards the maintenance of higher class public schools; furthermore, no pupil was to be admitted until he had passed the fifth standard. The subjects to be taught must either be approved by the Department in a new section of the code headed 'Technical Schools', or else conform to the existing requirements of the Science and Art Department. But such schools would have an advantage over higher class schools in that school boards would be allowed a much wider discretion in the use of the school fund for maintenance purposes, including the expense of providing tools and apparatus; also, the Department was authorized to give grants in respect of such subjects as were not covered by the Science and Art Department, though not in respect of attendance. These powers, while purely permissive, were on the whole not ungenerous, but school boards had always been chary of providing higher class schools of any description so long as they could claim full grants for other kinds of public school.

The other development was somewhat more fruitful in its consequences. It related to the full-scale inquiry into secondary education undertaken by the Parker Departmental Committee in the course of its investigations. In 1886 the reformed Department had instituted the statutory annual inspection of all higher class public schools and the voluntary inspection of other similar schools. It was also proposed to establish a simultaneous leaving examination as a means of raising and equating the standard of secondary education given in these schools, and much of the initiative behind this move must be placed to the credit of George Chrystal, Professor of Mathematics in the University of Edinburgh. As examiner in his own particular subject, he conducted an experiment in the same year in twelve schools coming under his inspection, to test the possibility of instituting such an examination. His conclusions were that the establishment of an examination of this nature would not present insuperable difficulties, and as a consequence the Department in 1887 asked its other inspectors to investigate the matter more fully, with a view to testing the expediency of issuing a certificate to individual pupils as the result of a leaving examination. Undoubtedly this was one of the most momentous experiments in the history of Scottish education, for never before had a common standard been attempted, and greater publicity was given to the proposal by publishing a general report of this second inspection of higher class schools in the Department's annual report.

The universities, it is true, had, in imitation of Oxford and Cambridge, introduced so-called 'local examinations' into Scotland in an endeavour to supply a common test of attainment in schools: Edinburgh and St. Andrews in 1865, Glasgow in 1877, and Aberdeen in 1880; but these examinations were in no sense intended to test fitness for university entrance. Consequently, having no specific aim, they did not prosper and were chiefly taken by girls. In the meantime, the matter was referred to the Departmental Committee of Inquiry, which in its third report strongly recommended that, in order to give secondary schools more definiteness of aim, leaving examinations should at once be set on foot for granting certificates of proficiency to pupils educated at such schools. For the present, they advocated that these examinations should be conducted by the Department, the responsible authority for inspecting higher class and endowed schools, but subject to revision in the light of experience. At the same time they issued a salutary warning that great care should be taken not to impair freedom of teaching in these schools by requiring uniformity of methods.

The Parker Committee's other findings on secondary education were equally enlightened. They expressed the opinion that in this sphere the country should look mainly to schools specially appropriated to that work, an opinion somewhat out of keeping perhaps with the general trend of Scottish educational tradition. In the large cities it was immaterial whether the high schools came under the school board, as at Edinburgh, Glasgow and Aberdeen, or under a separate board of directors, as at Dundee. In the smaller burghs, however, the existing distribution of grants offered too strong a temptation for the school board to concentrate its attention on securing passes in the primary standards and specific subjects, to the consequent neglect of secondary education proper. Accordingly, they recommended grants for higher education in public secondary as well as in primary schools, even if such aid were made generally conditional on local contributions of a similar amount, but the criterion must be the general efficiency of the school and not the passing of standards. They believed, however, that the fees for public secondary education should be as high as could reasonably be afforded by the parents concerned, while special arrangements should be made for providing free education for very promising children of poor parents. They proposed that where this could not be covered by endowments or private liberality the Department should be empowered to allow a limited expenditure from the school fund for the purpose.

Moreover, if grants for higher class public schools should be sanctioned, they suggested that a certain proportion of free places should be reserved for competition among children from public primary schools. Likewise, any school district sending pupils to a higher class public school outside its own area should contribute proportionately to any rate necessary for its support, provided it was allowed representation on the board of management. On the other hand, once local government was organized on a county basis (as was then impending), the Committee recommended that special boards or committees should be established to take over secondary education in counties, or convenient districts such as smaller burghs, with limited powers of rating.

As regards rural areas, the Committee reiterated the familiar plea that in every parish a public school should be maintained capable of preparing its best pupils for the university, and that where necessary the teaching staff should be strengthened for the purpose. In very thinly populated districts, however, they advocated instead central secondary schools to which promising children might be sent and boarded at no great distance from home. Without wishing to discourage higher departments of primary schools, the committee deprecated undue competition with secondary schools and enunciated the principle that fees should in all cases be made to cover the larger part of the cost of higher instruction. Consequently, the Department should have powers to sanction fees above 9d per week in grant-aided schools. Finally, the Committee came to the conclusion that, in general, secondary schools should be organized under one headmaster solely responsible to the governing body for arranging the curriculum and appointing the staff.

The first result of the Parker Committee's recommendations was the definite institution of a leaving certificate examination by the Department in 1888. To begin with, passes were awarded in individual subjects at three levels—lower, higher and honours grade—and could be taken only by pupils in higher class schools, public or otherwise. Papers were set in six subjects: English (including history and geography), mathematics (including arithmetic), Latin, Greek, French and German. To avoid imposing too great a uniformity on the schools, they were purely general in character, that is, not based upon prescribed books. Such, indeed, they have always since remained. The examination was not made compulsory on any school nor was it intended to act as a substitute for inspection, although the Department in fact proposed to reduce inspection to the minimum in the case of schools which presented a reasonable number of candidates. Furthermore, several professional bodies accepted it in lieu of their own entrance requirements and it naturally possessed an inherent advantage over the multiplicity of other possible examinations, such as the various university locals, each based on different prescribed books. For these reasons it was rapidly adopted by practically all the higher class schools in Scotland. The lack of funds, which had prevented the Department from implementing the provision of the act of 1878 regarding inspection of higher class schools, obliged it to restrict the examination to such schools and also to charge a small fee for each paper taken, for the Departmental Committee's recommendation regarding the granting of state aid to secondary schools was not immediately fulfilled.

Meanwhile, in 1890, the Residue Grant (referred to under elementary education) was estimated to make available £60,000 for technical education 'within the meaning of the Technical Schools (Scotland) Act of 1887'. It is noteworthy that this money was put into the hands of the County Councils, for not only was it the first subsidy to higher education but it also implied that such education was more effectively dealt with at the county than at the parish level. So far as Scotland was concerned, however, two practical difficulties were encountered in the application of the grant to assist technical education. In the first place, it was uncertain whether any money might be given to any governing body other than a school board, and in the second, no definition of technical education had been given in the original enactment, a defect which had been remedied for England in the Technical Instruction Act of 1889.

Accordingly, an amending act, the Technical Instruction Amendment (Scotland) Act, was passed in 1892 defining the ways in which a local authority might make contributions for the purpose of technical education, the schools and institutions which might be benefited, and the nature of the instruction which might be provided. Considerable latitude was allowed, and, in addition to school boards, governing bodies constituted under the Educational Endowments Act of 1882, or indeed any body of managers approved by the Department, were admitted to participation. As in the English act, technical instruction might include instruction in the principles of science and art applicable to industries, and in the application of special branches of science and art to specific industries and employments (including modern languages and commercial and agricultural subjects), and manual instruction was defined as instruction in the use of tools, processes of agriculture, and modelling in clay, wood or other material. But even this elucidation had disappointing results, and in fact only one school board is said to have erected a technical school.

In the same year, however, the Equivalent Grant was responsible for diverting the sum of £60,000 to secondary education in Scotland. This was the first parliamentary aid given unreservedly for that purpose, though previously Science and Art Department grants had been available in a more restricted capacity. Under section 2 of the Education and Local Taxation Account (Scotland) Act of 1892 certain directions were given regarding the disposal of the money formerly devoted to freeing elementary education under section 22 of the Local Government Act of 1889, and the inclusion of secondary education under sub-section 1(*a*) was doubtless due to the Parker Committee's recommendation that it should receive assistance. The act laid down that the cost of inspecting higher class schools and of holding Leaving Certificate examinations should be defrayed as a first charge out of this money, and the Department was thus enabled to extend the examinations to ordinary state-aided schools in response to a popular demand. Under this head it was estimated that £3,300 would be required; the balance was to be employed in making provision for secondary education in urban and rural districts by assisting either public schools or endowed institutions managed under the provisions of any act of parliament or approved scheme.

In practice this meant any higher class school which was not purely privately conducted, and the question arose of how the outstanding £56,700 should be distributed. The Secretary for Scotland at once appointed a departmental committee under the chairmanship of the Earl of Elgin to investigate the problem. After taking evidence, the committee reported in the same year that in their opinion the school board area was too small for the effective administration of secondary education. At the same time, however, they considered that school boards should be represented on any advisory local committee that might be set up to guide the Department as to the best distribution of the available funds. Similarly, they thought that the County Councils, on account both of their representative character and of their administration of funds applicable to technical education from the Residue Grant, should also undoubtedly take part in any committee, and that the presence of an official of the Department would be of great service. Consequently, they recommended the appointment in each county of a committee, composed of equal numbers of representatives of the County Council and of the school boards in the county and including an H.M. Inspector nominated by the Department, to report to the Department on the existing provision for higher education in their area and on any deficiency. In particular, it was proposed that they should name schools or centres where additional provision for such education might be made with advantage, delimit the area to be served by particular institutions and consider the claims of secondary schools in the county, other than higher class public schools, for admission to a share in the grant and on what conditions. In the case of Edinburgh, Glasgow, Dundee and Aberdeen it was suggested that the Department should appoint special consultative committees.

In a minute of 11th August 1892 the Department implemented these recommendations more or less in their entirety. County secondary education committees, on the basis recommended by the Elgin Committee, were set up, and, in the case of the four large cities, burgh committees, with the addition of representatives of important local endowments, were to be appointed. This decision was an important step towards enlarging the area of educational administration, and an interesting point of policy laid down in the act itself was that grant-aid should be made conditional in any participating school upon transferring the control of settling the fees from the teachers to the managers, thereby bringing to an end the questionable custom of direct interest in pupils' fees which had long been the schoolmaster's prerogative. Objection was taken to the excessive centralization of control vested in the Department, and by an amending minute of May 1893 the latter agreed to distribute the whole grant among the committees in proportion to the density of population in their area. At the same time the burgh of Leith and the parish of Govan were added to the total, thus bringing the number of secondary education committees up to thirty-nine (33 county committees, 5 burgh and 1 parish).

The revised policy was, however, open to the objection that in many instances the greatest need of assistance was experienced in the thinly rather than the densely populated districts. Moreover, the whole scheme had the demerit of adding to the number of local authorities, already sufficiently complicated. In the majority of cases the direct local authority was the school board, but in default of a system of technical schools proper a number of higher class schools, on the score of giving technical instruction, claimed a share in the Residue Grant of 1890, and thus came indirectly under the control of the county and burgh councils, in whose hands the administration lay. Now they were to come under the jurisdiction of secondary education committees as well. The Department attempted to simplify the administrative position by empowering local authorities, in a minute of 1896, to transfer administration of the Residue Grant for technical education to the secondary education committees, but despite the provision for increased representation on the latter, many local authorities were jealous of their rights and the response was only partial.

A further source of the dispersion of authority in the case of a number of higher class schools was the practice of claiming grants from the Science and Art Department at South Kensington. These were administered along somewhat the same lines as those for specific subjects, and in the ordinary way a considerable share went to schools under the code. From 1872, however, the Department had sanctioned so-called 'organized science schools' managed by a local committee, and five of these had grown up in Scotland, perhaps the most important being Allan Glen's, Glasgow. In addition, no less than thirty-five higher class schools claimed grants for special instruction in science and art and thus served still another master. Accordingly, in 1897, it was agreed to transfer, as from 1st April 1898, the administration of the Scottish share of the Science and Art grant from South Kensington to the Scotch Education Department.

In 1899 science was admitted as a subject for the Leaving Certificate examination, and in 1900 the system of grants was modified to allow average attendance to count as the basis of calculation. In 1903 only a 'reasonable number' of the pupils for whom grant was claimed were required to attend all the requisite instruction in experimental science and drawing, and finally in 1907 the whole work of the school, provided due provision was made in the curriculum for the teaching of science and art, was constituted the criterion for these grants. In 1898 a further sum of £35,000 was made available for the encouragement of secondary and technical (including agricultural) education by the Local Taxation Account (Scotland) Act of that year. The administration of this money was left in the hands of the Department, and as a first charge on it £2,000 was set aside for the increased cost of inspecting higher class public schools and conducting the Leaving Certificate examinations. A further £2,000 was devoted to agricultural education, and the balance was utilized for providing qualified teachers and adequate equipment for encouraging the teaching of science in secondary and technical schools not in receipt of grants under the code. All applications for a share in this 'Secondary and Technical Education Grant', as it came to be called, were, however, to be submitted to the Department through the Secondary

Education Committees. Thus by 1898 it was estimated that, exclusive of the specific subjects taught in schools under the code, some £200,000 was available annually for subsidizing secondary education.

As a consequence of the increased educational expenditure resulting from the Education Act of 1902 in England and Wales, Scotland was given a 'general aid grant' of about £230,000 a year, and from 1906 certain sums were made over from this to the secondary education committees to assist deserving pupils, particularly in outlying districts, to obtain a secondary education by means of bursaries and maintenance allowances. By this time the need for consolidating legislation to sort out the tangled administrative problems of education was clamant and action could not be long delayed. Meanwhile, the Department did what it could to exercise a unifying influence upon the secondary education of the country by introducing gradual changes into the Leaving Certificate examination. Up to this time the examinations might be taken by candidates of any age and in any order, almost without restriction, and were thus merely tests of proficiency in isolated subjects. Furthermore, the system led to a multiplicity of individual certificates granted by the Department for each pass. As an experiment the latter instituted a group certificate in 1900. This was made compulsory two years later and certificates for individual subjects were henceforth to be discontinued. The new group certificate was still awarded for proficiency in the individual subjects tested, but certain definite restrictions and minimum requirements were laid down. Four years' attendance at a recognized school, for instance, was a preliminary requirement before candidates might take the examination, and every group must comprise either at least four passes on the higher grade or three on the higher and two on the lower grade. English on the higher grade and mathematics on at least the lower were made compulsory, and where more than one language was taken, as an alternative to science, one of them had to be Latin.

In 1906 the Leaving Certificate was pegged to the Intermediate Certificate, as the successful completion of a post-intermediate course, and further changes were necessitated. These were successively the abolition of the honours grade in 1907 as liable to cause over-pressure, and the adoption of a 'curriculum' certificate in 1908, that is to say, an examination designed to test the curriculum offered as an organic whole rather than merely a group test of individual subjects. For this purpose teachers' estimates of candidates' probable success or failure on the basis of their class-work were to be taken into account (as was already done in the case of science), and high proficiency in one subject was allowed to compensate for slight weakness in another towards the award of a group certificate. In 1911 the Department relaxed the requirements still further by reducing the minimum group to three passes on the higher standard and one on the lower. At the same time, however, a post-intermediate course of not less than two years was required from all candidates, thus involving at least five years' attendance after completing the qualifying examination. In addition greater stringency in the subjects which might be offered was prescribed; the three higher passes had to comprise English (including history), either mathematics or science, and a language other than English.

Eventually legislation was secured, in December 1908, and the Education Act of that year, though it did not finally put secondary education in Scotland on a thoroughly satisfactory footing, did at least achieve a good deal in that direction. All the miscellaneous grants by which it had previously been financed were consolidated in a central fund, and the local distribution was canalized in a single district education fund to be administered by the secondary education committees. The latter thus received statutory recognition as the sole local authority for financing the higher education of a district, while the school boards were also reminded of their responsibilities to such schools as were managed by them. The anomalous term 'higher class public school' was superseded in the act by the more acceptable designation of secondary school, and any school board having the management of such a school was bound to maintain it in a condition of efficiency. For this purpose the school boards were at last authorized to utilize the school fund to the same extent as for any other public school under their management. In this way the doubt as to how far a school board was entitled to maintain a secondary school out of the school rate was finally settled.

In view of the increased powers conferred by the act upon the secondary education committees of each county the Department reconstituted their composition by a minute of August 1909. Previously county (or burgh) councils and the school board(s) had received equal representation on these committees, but for the future the specially elected educational element in each committee was to predominate. This was in line with the policy which culminated ten years later in the establishment of *ad hoc* education authorities on a county basis.

CHAPTER IX

TEACHER TRAINING BEFORE 1906

THE professional training of teachers is almost entirely a nineteenth century development in educational practice. Previously the parochial and burgh schoolmasters of Scotland were generally men who had received part of their education in one or other of the Scottish universities, though only a relatively small percentage were graduates. Consequently, they were usually competent scholars in their way, but it was not thought necessary to give them any instruction in the best methods of conveying what they knew to those who were to be their pupils. The necessity for some measure of professional training for intending teachers seems to have been first acutely felt in England as a result of the monitorial system established there by Bell and Lancaster at the beginning of the century. No systematic provision of training facilities was made, but as early as 1805 some instruction in the duties of taking over new schools was made available to selected monitors at Lancaster's model school in the Borough Road, and similar action was taken soon afterwards in connection with the two model schools conducted on Bell's Madras system at Baldwin's Gardens, Holborn, and the Barrington School at Bishop Auckland.

In Scotland the need was most pressing in the large towns, which, so far as elementary education was concerned, were outside the scope of the parochial system and were thus without the benefit of a supply of educated schoolmasters. The credit of being the first to give the matter serious consideration belongs to David Stow, who, like his predecessors, began by preparing his teachers (or 'trainers', as he preferred to call them) in the model infant school at Glasgow from 1826 onwards. But his systematic and philosophical treatment of the problem was far superior to the mechanical methods employed in the monitorial model schools. As early as 1827 the success of his efforts caused the education committee of the Church of Scotland to utilize Wood's Sessional School in Edinburgh for the same purpose. In the meantime the reformed Glasgow Educational Society began to project a full-scale training college, or normal seminary as it was called, and launched a public appeal for funds. In 1835 they appointed as rector John McCrie, son of the biographer of John Knox, and in the following year the buildings of the Glasgow Normal Seminary were begun at Dundas Vale. The new college was eventually opened on 31st October 1837, and in the same year the General Assembly of the Church of Scotland formally recognized the Edinburgh sessional school, in which a definite training department had been established in 1835, as 'The Normal and Sessional School of Edinburgh'.

Stow's own idea had been that a training college should be concerned mainly with professional training and not with the general education of the students. Circumstances, however, necessitated the development of the instructional side of the work in view of the lack of such educational facilities elsewhere. He had also intended that the new venture should be national and undenominational, but here again his hopes were frustrated on account of lack of funds. From the first the Dundas Vale training college was heavily in debt, as the Society's resources had been exhausted even before the completion of the buildings.

While still an assistant Poor Law Commissioner, Dr. James Kay, later first secretary to the Committee of Council on Education, had visited both the Glasgow

Normal Seminary and the General Assembly's Normal and Sessional School in Edinburgh. Impressed by what he saw there he also visited similar institutions on the Continent, and on his appointment as Secretary to the Committee of Council in 1839 endeavoured to set up a state normal school with a sum of £10,000, voted by Parliament for the erection of model schools but not yet utilized. Owing to sectarian opposition the project failed to materialize and the best Kay could do was have the money divided equally between the two English denominational societies by a minute of 3rd June 1839. However, in conjunction with E. C. Tufnell, he opened his own training college at Battersea in 1840; it was residential in character and was conducted on undenominational lines until 1843, when it was taken over by the National Society on account of financial stringency. The opening of the National Society's St. Mark's College, Chelsea, in 1841, and of the British and Foreign School Society's new training college in the Borough Road in 1842 set the training of teachers in England on a firm basis.

As early as 1839 Stow had appealed to the Committee of Council for a grant to wipe out the existing debt at Dundas Vale, but Kay, although sympathetic, was unable to persuade his committee for the same reasons that he had encountered difficulty with his own plans. However, in 1841 an agreement was reached whereby a grant of £5,000 (equivalent to those made to the English societies) should be given towards reducing the debt and an annual recurrent sum of £500 be paid towards maintenance, provided the management of the college was transferred to the Church of Scotland and the General Assembly contributed the same amount.

In this way, as in England, the training of teachers was placed in the first instance on a denominational basis and the Church of Scotland had a training college unexpectedly thrust upon it. This move encouraged the General Assembly to appeal in turn for a grant to set their own normal school in Edinburgh on a satisfactory footing. In 1843 a further grant of £5,000 was authorized for the erection of a new Church of Scotland Training College in Edinburgh, but the occurence of the Disruption in the same year held up the proceedings and it was not until 1845 that this second college was opened in Johnston Terrace. In Glasgow, Stow and the majority of his staff joined the Free Church and in consequence found themselves ousted from their positions, despite the fact that officially the college was still open to students of all denominations. As in the case of the schools, the Free Church Education Committee felt obliged to make provision for those who had been displaced, and on 8th May 1845 Stow and his colleagues were accommodated in temporary premises until a new college, towards which the Privy Council contributed £3,000, was opened at Cowcaddens in the following year.

Not content with this measure of emulation, the Free Church decided also to set up a training college in Edinburgh, and a further grant of £3,000 was obtained from the Committee of Council for the purpose. With this money Moray House, formerly the residence of the Earls of Moray, was acquired and adapted to the needs of a training college in 1848. Thus the Disruption was indirectly responsible for the extension of facilities for the training of teachers as well as of provision for the education of children. In the main the duplication of training colleges in Edinburgh and Glasgow was not unfortunate in its results. It produced a healthy rivalry without undue sectarian bitterness, and although appointments to the staffs of the colleges were on a denominational basis, students frequented those of either Church indiscriminately. The four colleges were on the same pattern, non-residential and at first open to men only, but in 1849 grants were made available to women also, and they became co-educational.

The movement for teacher-training was for long confined purely to elementary teachers, and it had the unfortunate effect of introducing a dichotomy within the profession. It was greatly enhanced by Kay-Shuttleworth's famous minute of 25th August 1846, which created the pupil-teacher system. In Scotland it might have been possible to utilize the educational resources of the country to educate intending teachers at the easily accessible universities and reserve the training colleges for professional training, as Stow had hoped. In England this was out of the question and Kay-Shuttleworth was faced with the problem both of keeping the training colleges solvent and of assuring a constant supply of qualified entrants. In order, therefore, to keep a sufficient number of promising children at school, he allowed certain recognized schools to select some of their better pupils about the age of 13 for a 5-years' apprenticeship. During this period they were to help with the work of teaching, for which they received a small remuneration, and at the same time to continue their own education for 1½ hours daily under the tuition of the headmaster, who was also to be remunerated for the extra work involved.

At the end of their apprenticeship pupil-teachers were eligible to compete for Queen's Scholarships tenable at a training college under inspection. The training colleges also received capitation grants for each Queen's Scholar in training, the grant in respect of women being two-thirds that of men. To make the teaching profession more attractive, the minute provided that certificated teachers trained in this way should receive annual grants as increments to their salary and be eligible for a pension on their retirement. The financial stimulus of the capitation grants led to the erection of a considerable number of new denominational training colleges in England but had little effect in Scotland. In 1850, however, the Episcopal Church of Scotland established a small residential training college for men at Croft-an-Righ House, Holyrood, Edinburgh.

Unlike the other Scottish colleges it did not become co-educational, and in 1867, after the official recognition of female teachers by the Parochial and Burgh Schools Act of 1861, it was converted into a college for women students; it was transferred to Dalry House ten years later.

The pupil-teacher system continued practically unmodified until the passing of the Education Act of 1872 and indeed for long after that. One grave weakness of the scheme was that those who failed to gain Queen's Scholarships and who could not afford to take the training college course without financial assistance, simply went on teaching, in spite of their lack of training. They were even encouraged to do so, for in the summer of 1848 the Committee of Council instituted a common examination for certification which conferred the privileges granted by the minute of 1846 and allowed practising teachers who had never been at a training college to enter for it *pari passu* with students completing their training. The period of apprenticeship was also reduced to four years, and a further dilution in the supply of trained teachers was caused by the fact that an appreciable number of those who entered the training colleges utilized them merely for the purpose of general education. To check this tendency it became necessary for the Committee of Council to limit its grants to 75% of the actual expenditure of the training colleges in Scotland. Otherwise, they prospered well enough until the act of 1872 assured them of a greatly increased demand for teachers. They were spared the anxious period imposed upon their sister institutions in England by the Revised Code, under which a policy of drastic retrenchment in training grants, salary increments and teachers' pensions was inaugurated.

At the same time, many prospective teachers continued to pass through the universities as before, but although the five training colleges were distributed between two of the university cities of the country, no attempt was at first made to combine the work of the two agencies. As early as 1865 H.M. Inspector for the North-East, Dr. John Kerr, fearing a decline in the scholarship of the teachers in the Dick Bequest area of Aberdeenshire, Banff and Moray, who had formerly been nearly all graduates, outlined a scheme for combining university education with normal school training. In this he was ably seconded by Mr. S. S. Laurie, who was not only the Dick Bequest's visitor in these counties but, as Secretary to the Church of Scotland's Education Committee, had a powerful influence over the two training colleges in Edinburgh and Glasgow. So long, however, as Scotland remained tied to England under the Education Department no such scheme was adopted.

The Education Act of 1872 brought some expansion to the Scottish system of teacher-training. Anticipating the necessity for an increased supply of teachers to implement the act, the Church of Scotland immediately pressed for the establishment of a training college in Aberdeen. This was agreed to by the Department but limited to women students, and the new college was opened in 1873. In the following year the Free Church, as was its custom, followed suit by establishing another training college there, also for women. In 1879 the numbers at the Church of Scotland College in Johnston Terrace, Edinburgh, had become so great that the Education Committee opened a new college in Chambers Street and transferred the men students there. From then on the Edinburgh college was operated in two wings, in which the sexes were segregated, but continued to be supervised by the same staff of lecturers.

The first Scotch Code of 1873 also introduced the policy of combined training by permitting Queen's scholars in training colleges, by article 102 (*c*), to attend not more than two university classes prescribed for graduation in Arts or Science during each of the two years of their attendance at college. Unfortunately, it did not make any provision for allowing matriculation and class fees to count as legitimate expenditure for grant-aid, and in consequence only 33 students took advantage of the scheme in the first year of its operation. This anomaly was, however, rectified five years later and the number of students rose to 171 in 1879. In practice the arrangement was limited to Edinburgh and Glasgow because no training facilities as yet existed at St. Andrews, and those in Aberdeen were restricted to women, then not accepted as university students. Owing to a disparity in the length of the training college course of two years as against the minimum graduation course of three years, it was not possible for such students to proceed to a degree. To meet their special case, however, the two universities instituted in 1880 the diploma of 'Literate in Arts' (L.A.), which was conferred on any candidate who after two years' attendance at the university had taken the degree examinations in four of the seven Arts subjects qualifying for M.A. and passed a satisfactory test in a fifth subject of his own choice. The literateship was not a degree and in consequence was not greatly sought after, but it represented a sincere attempt on the part of the universities to give token recognition to those intending teachers who took the combined course.

Another development in the sphere of teacher-training which resulted, if indirectly, from the Education Act of 1872 was the establishment of chairs of education at the Universities of Edinburgh and St. Andrews in 1876. The act having madc statutory provision in other educational fields formerly assisted by a residue fund left over from the estate of the Rev. Dr. Andrew Bell in 1832, the trustees were somewhat at a loss to know how to use the funds at their disposal. Bell was the founder of the so-called 'Madras system' of education, one of the variants of the monitorial system, and though his fame and active educational work were chiefly confined to England, he was a Scot by birth and upbringing, and left a considerable sum of money for the furtherance of Scottish education. The residue fund was not a large one, but the trustees resolved to set aside the sum of £10,000 for the purpose of endowing a chair of education at Edinburgh as a means of perpetuating the founder's educational theories. Subsequently, Dr. Bell's connection with St. Andrews caused them to divert £4,000 of the original sum towards establishing a chair there also. They expected the Treasury to supplement the income from the capital sum, as was customary in the case of new chairs in Scottish universities, by an annual grant of £200, but this hope did not, unfortunately, materialize. The result was that the new chairs were from the outset gravely handicapped on account both of their anomalous position and of their inadequate endowment, particularly in the case of St. Andrews.

The intention of the Bell trustees was that the professors should give instruction to prospective teachers taking the whole of their academic education at the university, but the Department still required all candidates for certification to take the annual government examination. This requirement acted as a considerable deterrent in the sphere of primary education, where a large number of the available posts, being the headships of rural schools, necessitated possession of a government certificate, for which the training colleges from long practice were more expert at preparing candidates, but it was less important in the sphere of secondary education. It was therefore in the preparation of teachers for the higher class public schools that the new chairs at first did their best work, and, notwithstanding the rather discouraging conditions under which they were expected to operate, two outstanding first occupants were found. The Bell trustees reserved the right of making these appointments and selected Mr. S. S. Laurie, Secretary to the Church of Scotland Education Committee, for the Edinburgh chair and Mr. J. M. D. Meiklejohn, a well-known writer of school text-books, for that at St. Andrews. No happier choice could have been made in either case.

The Universities of Aberdeen and St. Andrews resented their exclusion from the system of combined training which operated at Edinburgh and Glasgow, and repeatedly pressed for the approval of some similar scheme in their own case. No action was taken about St. Andrews, but in 1885 the two Aberdeen training colleges were permitted by the Department to admit a limited number of men students, provided the latter were in attendance at classes in the University. In 1886 the University of Edinburgh instituted a post-graduate 'Schoolmaster's Diploma' of two types—a general diploma for pass graduates and a secondary diploma for graduates with honours—under the supervision of the chair of education. For a number of years this diploma remained a purely academic distinction but eventually in 1896 it was recognized by the Department for purposes of certification, and led to similar provision being made at Glasgow and Aberdeen.

Since the universities were still restricted to male students and the existing training colleges prepared their candidates chiefly for elementary schools, there was an obvious lack of a training centre for women students intending to become teachers in secondary schools. To meet this need, St. George's College was opened in Edinburgh in 1886. It presented women students for the examinations of the Teachers' Training Syndicate of the University of Cambridge, in which it achieved considerable success. Since the demand was necessarily limited, however, a girls' high school was started in connection with it in 1888, and the college was carried on as a training department. After 1892, when women were admitted to the Scottish universities, a number of its students preferred to take the Edinburgh University schoolmaster's diploma. In a denominational training system another noteworthy lack was the absence of a training college for Roman Catholic students. Strangely, this want was not met until 1895, when a Roman Catholic training college for women was opened in Glasgow at Dowanhill. Like its Episcopal counterpart in Edinburgh, this college was entirely residential, but it should be noted that residential facilities for women students had in the meantime been provided at the Church of Scotland and Free Church colleges in Edinburgh, and at the Church of Scotland colleges in Glasgow and Aberdeen.

The recognition of the university classes in the theory and history of education at Edinburgh and St. Andrews as qualifying for graduation in Arts, under an ordinance of the Scottish Universities Commission in 1892, greatly enhanced the academic standing of the chairs of education and stimulated the foundation of lectureships in education at Aberdeen in 1893 and Glasgow in 1894. There was still, however, no satisfactory scheme for linking up university education with professional training at St. Andrews, nor was there a single training college at Dundee, although in each of the other three large cities there was a duplication of such provision. Therefore, the Scottish Universities Commissioners carefully considered representations on the subject from the St. Andrews University Court, the Council of Dundee University College and the Dundee School Board.

The English code of 1890 had authorized the establishment of what were known as 'Day Training Colleges' in connection with the universities and university colleges in England, and it was proposed to institute something of the sort at St. Andrews and Dundee. The so-called Day Training Colleges were the outcome of the recommendations of a Royal Commission under Viscount Cross which had sat from 1886 to 1888 to inquire into the working of the elementary education acts in England and Wales. They had found that the existing colleges were too exclusively residential in character, too strictly sectarian, too expensive financially, and insufficient in number to accommodate all the candidates who had passed the Queen's Scholarship examination. They therefore recommended that training departments should be established in the university institutions of England and Wales, undenominational and non-residential in nature, as a means of increasing the available accommodation in the most economic manner.

None of these reasons, however, was applicable to Scotland, for the training colleges there were neither residential nor narrowly sectarian although managed by the Presbyterian churches. Moreover, the Departmental Committee under Mr. C. S. Parker had reported in 1888 that their cost to the state was moderate, and the universities commissioners themselves found that the existing colleges were not fully attended. Accordingly, while fully conscious of the importance of enabling as many students as possible to receive their training in the universities, they were not prepared to recommend the establishment of university training departments on the same scale as in England. They did, however, propose to the Department in 1893 that a certain number of intending teachers, qualified by their previous education, should be admitted to the universities on the same footing as other students, and at the same time receive the same financial assistance as students taking training college or combined courses. On the other hand, the commissioners recommended that there should be no modification of the university system for the special benefit of these students, except that they should be required to attend the classes of the Professor of Education. They also considered that if any such arrangement were made it should not be confined to St. Andrews and Dundee but be open to be shared by the other universities as well.

The fruit of these recommendations was to be found

in the Scotch code of 1895, which established the system of 'Queen's Students' (not to be confused with Queen's Scholars). Under article 83 any Scottish university or university college was authorized to set up a local committee to supervise the training of students who had passed the university preliminary examination or held equivalent Leaving Certificates. These students were to receive their academic education in university classes and the local committee was to be responsible for furnishing the means of their professional training. Both the students and the local committees received a capitation grant, and on completion of their training candidates were examined by a joint board of university professors and H.M. Inspectors. Some responsibility for the training of teachers was thus shifted from the churches to the universities (though it was still under the general surveillance of the Department), but the response was less enthusiastic than might have been expected. St. Andrews and Aberdeen immediately set up local committees; in 1900 Dundee University College also availed itself of the opportunity of taking Queen's Students and appointed Mr. J. S. Malloch Lecturer in Education; and finally in 1903 Glasgow followed suit, but no local committee was ever established at Edinburgh.

In the meantime, the Department had in 1901 relaxed a certain amount of its control over the training colleges by permitting them to draw up their own courses of education and training, and to conduct their own examination of candidates for certification in lieu of the annual government examination. This was undoubtedly a token of confidence in the existing system and the efficient conduct of the training colleges under the management of the churches. Nevertheless, there was something inconsistent in taking over the schools and yet leaving the training of teachers in the hands of voluntary agencies. In consequence, the Department entered into negotiations with the churches in order to place the training of teachers on a national basis, and on 30th January 1905 an important minute was issued, superseding all previous arrangements.

By this minute the country was divided into four so-called 'provinces', based upon the university cities of St. Andrews, Glasgow, Aberdeen and Edinburgh, and in future the training of all teachers in each province was to be placed under a 'provincial committee', representative of the various interests in the area which it covered. Both the Church of Scotland and the denomination known after 1900 as the 'United Free Church' (formed by the union of the United Presbyterian with the former Free Church) agreed to hand over their training colleges to these new committees, but the smaller Episcopal college in Edinburgh and the Roman Catholic college in Glasgow declined to enter into any agreement in the matter. The size of the committees varied from 22 in the St. Andrews province to 38 in the Glasgow province, but in general similar interests were represented. In the case of the Glasgow, Aberdeen and Edinburgh provinces, provision was made for the representation of any church or denomination from which a training college had been transferred, by the co-optation of an agreed number of members. Otherwise, the principal interests involved were the University Courts, central institutions (such as technical colleges, art schools, etc.), the school boards, the secondary school managers, and (as co-opted members) practising teachers. In each case an H.M. Chief Inspector was to act as the Department's assessor on the committee, and the number of members from each source was carefully specified in a schedule to the minute, which outlined the composition of the individual committees.

CHAPTER X

THE UNIVERSITIES SINCE 1889

THE Universities (Scotland) Act of 1889 was divided into three parts, dealing with the constitution or reconstitution of statutory bodies, the appointment of an executive commission to carry out the provisions and the redemption of certain ancient charges on the Crown. One of the major reforms was the reconstitution of all the University Courts somewhat along the lines suggested by the Royal Commission of 1876. In each case the number of General Council assessors was increased from one to four, and the experiment of including two civic representatives was extended to the other three universities besides Edinburgh.

In general, the four University Courts were assimilated as regards size and composition, but there were certain minor differences between them. Thus, the number of Senatus representatives was likewise increased from one to four, except at St. Andrews, where only three Senatus assessors were authorized, but the Principal of St. Mary's College was made an *ex officio* member and the Principal of the United College was to be in future recognized as Principal of the University. Provision was even made for the inclusion of the Principal of Dundee University College, 'if and when the said college shall be affiliated to and made to form part of the University'. Similarly, the civic representatives in each case were to be the Lord Provost of the relative city and an assessor nominated by the Town Council, but again at St. Andrews there was a difference, namely that they should be the Provosts of St. Andrews and Dundee. The other existing members, such as the Rector, the Principal and the assessors nominated by the Chancellor and Rector, were retained, but at Glasgow the Dean of Faculties was dropped from membership of the University Court. The enlarged Courts thus had fourteen members (fifteen at St. Andrews after the inclusion of the Principal of Dundee University College), but up to four additional representatives of any colleges affiliated under the provisions of the act were sanctioned in each case, above the statutory number.

The whole revenue and property of the university was transferred by the act from the Senatus Academicus and vested in the reconstituted University Court. A Scottish Universities Committee of the Privy Council was also constituted under the act, in spite of the opinion of the Royal Commission of 1876 that such a step would be impracticable. It was to consist of the Lord President of the Council, the Secretary for Scotland, at least one member of the judicial committee of the Privy Council, the Lord Justice-General, the Lord Justice-Clerk, the Lord Advocate, the four Chancellors and the four Rectors, provided they were members of the Privy Council; and such other members of the Privy Council as might be from time to time appointed.

The powers and duties of the University Court, Senatus Academicus and General Council were redefined. In addition to administering and managing the property of the university, the Court was now required to review decisions of the Senatus Academicus and also to take into consideration all representations made to it by that body and by the General Council. It was to continue to appoint professors whose chairs might be in the patronage of the university, examiners and lecturers, and to grant recognition of extra-mural teaching for purposes of graduation. It might take proceedings against any member of staff without the necessity of anyone outside its membership appearing as a prosecutor. Finally, it was given the power of founding all new professorships, subject to the approval of the Scottish Universities Committee of the Privy Council, and in future no new professorships were to be founded except in this way. Thus, at last, a check on the indiscriminate founding of new chairs was introduced, although the machinery was to prove somewhat cumbersome. The Senatus Academicus was to continue to regulate and superintend teaching and discipline and might appoint two-thirds of the members of any standing committee on libraries and museums belonging to the university. The General Council was empowered to hold special meetings at the instance of the Chancellor, in addition to the statutory half-yearly meetings, and might appoint committees to report on any matter remitted to them by the full Council. As a result of this, most of the work of the General Councils is now carried on by a small business committee.

The act also set up, as in 1858, an executive commission of sixteen members, under the chairmanship of Lord Kinnear, to adjudicate in a number of important matters. Its powers were originally in force until 1st January 1892, but they might be continued by order in council and were eventually extended for six years beyond that date. This was occasioned largely by the difficulty of effecting the incorporation, implicit in the provisions of the act, of Dundee University College in the University of St. Andrews. Altogether two hundred and fifty-one meetings of the commissioners were held, and undoubtedly they performed their task with an efficiency quite as commendable as that of their predecessors thirty years earlier.

The powers of the commissioners were defined in section 14 of the Act, and, with certain modifications necessitated by changed conditions, they were very similar to those conferred on the previous executive commission set up under the act of 1858. A good deal was left to their discretion, but the following were the chief matters recommended for the commissioners' attention. They were to have power to regulate endowments and bursaries in operation for more than twenty-five years at the passing of the act, and to transfer to the University Court the patronage of professorships in the hands of private individuals or corporate bodies other than the curators of patronage of the University of Edinburgh. They might regulate the powers, duties and privileges of university officers, and abolish professorships or other offices that should appear unnecessary to them. They could regulate the composition and number of the Faculties, alter the designation of professorships, and create new Faculties.

They were given wide powers regarding the admission of students, particularly in respect of the amount and appropriation of the fees to be charged; the course of study, length of the academic year and the appointment of examiners; the granting of degrees and the institution of new degrees; and the establishment of a preliminary examination. The question of the admission of women to graduation and provision for their instruction in one or more Faculties was also left to their discretion. They were further charged with the duty of regulating the salaries of principals, professors, lecturers and assistants, of founding new professorships or lectureships where necessary, of determining the conditions and scale of pensions for principals and professors after the passing of the act, and of laying down regulations for the constitution and functions of a Students' Representative Council in each university. Finally, they were empowered, though in this matter they took no action, to establish after 1st January 1892, or on the expiration of their powers, a general University Court of the four universities of the kind suggested in the report of the commission of 1876-8, for reviewing the general interests of the universities, especially in regard to degrees and examinations. In spite of this omission, however, the four University Courts have occasionally taken concerted action on such questions.

Under section 15 of the act the commissioners were authorized to extend any of the universities by making ordinances for the affiliation of new colleges, provided they obtained the consent of both parties to the project. Apparently the nature of such affiliations might be only temporary, since the relative ordinances might afterwards be rescinded by the University Court with the approval of the Scottish Universities Committee of the Privy Council. The special case of St. Andrews University and Dundee University College was individually, if ambiguously, dealt with in the following section. Here the commissioners were given power 'to affiliate the said university college to and make it form part of the said university, with the consent of the university court of St. Andrews and also of the said college, with the object, *inter alia*, of establishing a fully equipped conjoint university school of medicine', but were also enjoined to have due regard to existing interests and to the aims and constitution of the University College as set forth in the trust-deed. In practice this proved a ticklish problem.

Section 17 abolished the remaining vestiges of university tests, and sections 20 and 21 laid down the procedure for making ordinances. Those made or approved by the commissioners themselves were to be published for four consecutive weeks in the *Edinburgh Gazette* and after lying on the tables of both Houses of Parliament for twelve weeks might be approved by the Queen in Council provided no legitimate objection were taken to them. With additional safeguards, a similar procedure was required of University Courts making new ordinances after the expiration of the commissioners' powers. The written consent of the Chancellor to any proposed alterations was no longer required, but the University Court was now obliged to communicate the draft not only to its own Senatus Academicus and General Council for their opinion, but also to the University Courts of the other three universities, before submitting it for parliamentary approval. Thus, any other University Court which might consider its interests in any way affected by the draft ordinance might lodge objections with the Scottish Universities Committee of the Privy Council. There can be little doubt that this unwieldy method has increased the conservatism already endemic in the Scottish universities and made them on the whole unduly resistant to change. Lastly, an annual sum of £42,000 was put at the disposal of the commissioners to enable them to carry out their reforms with adequate financial assistance, but it was expressly stated that, apart from any sums previously granted out of public monies towards the endowment of a chair, no portion of this grant was to be applied to any chair in the Faculty of Theology. The restriction was not, however, held to affect any chair of Hebrew or oriental languages.

The commissioners issued one hundred and sixty-nine ordinances, all of which were approved by order in council (except that one was subsequently withdrawn in favour of an amending ordinance). In addition, they published a number of regulations and declarations regarding elections of assessors and the reconstitution of University Courts. In the absence of explicit instructions in the act itself they mistakenly incorporated under this latter head the agreement reached between Dundee University College and St. Andrews University in an order dated 21st March 1890, whereas the correct procedure would have been to issue an ordinance. Certain parties opposed on principle to the affiliation successfully challenged this oversight in the law courts but it was afterwards rectified by including the original agreement in an ordinance subsequently approved. Thus on 15th January 1897 Dundee University College was eventually affiliated to and made to form part of the University of St. Andrews on the terms mutually agreed, except that, on the recommendation of the Scottish Universities Committee of the Privy Council, a clause authorizing the election of two representatives of the college on the University Court was struck out before the ordinance was finally approved.

By the terms of the agreement the union thus effected was to be dissoluble only by act of parliament, while the University College, though generally under the control of the University Court, was to retain its original constitution. This provided for an education board composed of professors, a council responsible for the financial solvency of the college, and a rather ill-defined court of governors presided over by the college president. The appointment of members of the teaching staff was vested in the University Court and the professors were made members of the Senatus Academicus of St. Andrews University. But the college council retained the patronage of the principalship and continued to appoint its own administrative staff. Such an untidy arrangement inevitably opened up the way to future discord, and a further complicating factor was the conjoint medical school set up in terms of section 16 of the act. Though situated in Dundee, it had no organic connection with the University College, which still taught at the pre-clinical stage, and came directly under the control of the University Court. The pre-clinical teaching facilities, rather against the advice of the commissioners themselves, were duplicated at St. Andrews by a reorganization of resources, but the clinical teaching was necessarily confined to Dundee.

A major change effected by the ordinances of the commissioners was the admission in June 1892 of women to graduation in any Faculty, at the discretion of the University Court, on practically the same terms as men. Previously, all the Scottish universities had shown themselves sympathetic to the movement for the higher education of women by the establishment, between 1868 and 1877, of associations for the university education of women. They had no power in law to grant women degrees[1] but they did what they could by way of compromise in offering instruction and examinations specially provided for women. Courses of lectures in the more usual Arts subjects were delivered by the professors at each of the universities, although at Aberdeen and St. Andrews they had to be discontinued for lack of students.

As already explained, the 'local examinations', instituted between 1865 and 1880 in imitation of Oxford and Cambridge, were of great service in testing the education of girls at the secondary level, and in 1879 the University of Glasgow followed the example of Cambridge in establishing a higher local examination specially for the benefit of woman candidates. The University of Edinburgh went even further and, at a higher level still, began in 1874 to offer a special 'Certificate in Arts' which was awarded to women students who, after taking the special lecture courses provided for them, passed in three or more of the seven subjects required of men for the M.A. degree. In 1876 the University of St. Andrews, though no longer providing lecture courses for women, instituted the diploma of L.L.A. (Lady Literate in Arts), which could be taken by examination at local centres throughout the country. It enjoyed an enormous vogue in its time. Indeed, it was not discontinued until 1920, and between 1877 and 1918 the diploma was conferred on over 4,100 candidates. In these forty years the regulations were periodically changed, but latterly a pass was required in seven subjects, which were arranged in four departments.

[1] The courageous attempts to open the Edinburgh Medical School to women students, made by Miss Sophia Jex-Blake between 1869 and 1874, ended in failure.

These were language, philosophy, science and 'other subjects', but the alternative of a pass in five of them, and honours in a sixth, was also accepted. Every group must, however, include one subject from each of the first three departments of study.

The commissioners' ordinance sanctioning the admission of women to graduation in the normal way specifically stated that the instruction of women might be given either in mixed classes or separately. Three of the universities immediately adopted the first of these alternatives as being the more practicable, but the University of Glasgow, in the first instance, followed a different plan. In 1883 the Glasgow Association for the Higher Education of Women, originally founded in 1877, was incorporated as the 'Queen Margaret College'. In 1893, after the passing of the ordinance, this was transferred to the University as the Women's Department, and the principle of separate instruction was initiated there.[1] The college already had organized curricula in both Arts and Medicine and possessed eleven separate lectureships in these Faculties. From the beginning, however, mixed classes were necessary at the honours stage and gradually the policy of segregation began to break down. Eventually the practice extended to ordinary subjects as well, but the college remained a separate entity right up to 1935, when the last vestiges of the system finally disappeared. Co-education at all stages of education is an essential characteristic of the Scottish educational tradition.

Another question regarding the admission of students to the universities, which severely exercised the minds of the commissioners, was the expediency of instituting a

[1] At Edinburgh, however, women were not admitted to the Medical School, as distinct from graduation in medicine, until 1916. This difficulty was overcome by the establishment of a School of Medicine for women in 1886, founded by Dr. Jex-Blake after training in London and qualifying in Ireland. At first it led to the licentiateship of the Royal Colleges of Physicians and Surgeons in Edinburgh, later to the university's degrees, and it was finally discontinued on the admission of women to the normal courses for men.

preliminary examination before attendance should qualify for graduation. They were unwilling to debar promising students from the benefit of a university education simply because of the lack of a properly organized system of secondary education in the country, and at the same time they wished to maintain the distinction between school and university education. Ultimately they compromised. A preliminary examination requiring a pass in English and mathematics and two other subjects, of which one must be Latin or Greek, was adopted, but the commissioners urged the retention for the time being of the junior classes in Latin, Greek and mathematics, while expressing the opinion that such classes should not be a permanent part of the university equipment. As a concession to handicapped candidates the commissioners, though insisting on the successful completion of the preliminary examination before any examination qualifying for graduation might be taken, did permit attendance at qualifying classes by students with an incomplete group, provided the entrance requirements in respect of these particular classes were satisfied.

The commissioners introduced extensive changes within the system of graduation itself. In Arts they did not altogether abolish the old regulations for the ordinary degree of M.A., but, while retaining seven as the necessary number of subjects, they permitted *pari passu* with the existing curriculum certain options at the choice of the candidate. For convenience of reference they arranged all the qualifying courses in four departments with the following generic headings: (1) language and literature; (2) mental philosophy; (3) science; (4) history and law. They stipulated that of the seven necessary subjects four must be Latin or Greek, logic and metaphysics or moral philosophy, mathematics or natural philosophy, English or history or a modern language. They fixed the length of the Arts course at three winter sessions of twenty weeks, between the beginning of October and 10th April of the ensuing year, and prescribed one hundred class meetings on separate days for each qualifying course; but they also suggested the possibility of introducing a summer session of ten weeks beginning in May. This was difficult to enforce, however, since it was not provided for in the commissions of professors appointed before the approval of the ordinance by order in council.

The commissioners also set graduation with honours on a proper footing by discontinuing the obligation on candidates to go through the whole curriculum for the ordinary degree before proceeding to specialization. They introduced three grades of honours and considerably widened the choice of honours groups, outside of which they required attendance at only three subjects on the ordinary standard. The old natural science group was done away with, but in addition to the traditional groups in classics, philosophy and mathematics, new honours groups were instituted in English, modern languages, history, economic science, Semitic languages and Indian languages. The universities themselves by subsequent ordinances further modified these regulations in 1908 (or 1910 in the case of St. Andrews). The general effect was to introduce a greater measure of specialization into the ordinary degree by reducing the number of prescribed subjects to five (or six, where two subjects were deemed 'cognate') and requiring a second year of study in two of them. At the same time the number of outside subjects on the ordinary standard in an honours degree was also reduced to two, and the academic year was definitely divided into three terms, including at least twenty-five teaching weeks. An attempt was made to improve the standard of the teaching by reducing the number of class meetings to seventy-five and supplementing the formal lectures by 'tutorial' instruction.

In Medicine the commissioners extended the course

from four to five years and made graduation in both medicine and surgery simultaneously a necessary requirement of all candidates. For the old degree of C.M. (Master in Surgery) they substituted the degree of Ch.B. and introduced as a higher qualification in surgery, parallel to the doctorate in medicine, the degree of Ch.M. (Master of Surgery). In future both the M.D. and Ch.M. degrees were to be taken at a higher level than the double degree of M.B., Ch.B., partly by further examination and partly by thesis. Neither might be taken before the age of twenty-four, and at least one year's continued study, or two years' medical or surgical practice, was prescribed as a preliminary requirement.

In Science the commissioners noted with approval the practice at Edinburgh of delegating responsibility for supervising graduation in Science to a special committee of the Faculty of Arts, and to regularize the position they decided to create new Faculties of Science in all the universities. They also confirmed the practice of conferring the degrees of B.Sc. and D.Sc. in both pure and applied science. Regulations for the latter varied from one university to another in accordance with the facilities available, but the branches covered comprised engineering, agriculture and public health. In pure science, however, the commissioners were able to lay down a uniform curriculum of seven subjects (with certain options) to be taken in a course extending over three academic years. Three of these subjects had to be passed in a 'first science examination' and the remainder at a 'final science examination', in which the standard was to be as nearly as possible equivalent to that of the degree of M.A. with honours. The commissioners did not, however, authorize the award of honours in science, but they permitted special distinction to be awarded, where merited, in one or more subjects.

The degree of B.Sc. was thus something of a cross

between an ordinary and an honours degree, and after nearly thirty years' experience of the system the various universities took individual action in 1921 to have it changed in favour of a system more closely resembling that for graduation in Arts, by instituting graduation in Science at ordinary and honours levels. The commissioners limited the award of the D.Sc. degree in both pure and applied science to graduates of five years' standing, and abolished the practice of conferring it in mental science and philology. Instead, they established in Arts parallel higher degrees of D.Phil. and D.Litt., which might also be taken only by honours graduates of five years' standing. For all these doctorates a thesis was required which would be an original contribution to learning.

For graduation in Law the commissioners accepted the degree of LL.B., as established by their predecessors, restricted to graduates in Arts after a three years' course of study. But they introduced some alterations with a view to making the degree rather more professional and less academic in character. The possibility of fusing the degree with that in Arts by including in the latter one or two of the subjects from the department of history and law allowed of an increase in the number of subjects required for the LL.B. Full courses in civil law, Scots law and conveyancing were retained as before, but English law was allowed as an alternative to Scots law and political economy or mercantile law instead of conveyancing. Constitutional law and history was also retained and raised to the status of a full course. Compulsory half-courses in public international law (as previously) and in jurisprudence were laid down, and a choice of two further half-courses in international private law, political economy (if not already taken), administrative law or forensic medicine (previously compulsory) was left to the option of the candidate. The revised regulations thus prescribed four full and four half-courses as against three full and three half-courses under the former regulations. With some hesitation the commissioners also confirmed by ordinance the practice at Edinburgh and Glasgow of granting a first degree in law by establishing the degree of B.L. (Bachelor of Law) in all the universities where teaching facilities for it existed. As before, this remained partly an Arts degree until 1911, when the four University Courts made it a purely Law degree by increasing the number of Law subjects required, though these were still less numerous than for the post-graduate LL.B.

In the case of Divinity the commissioners regretted their inability to remodel the Faculty or make any material improvement in its position. In all the universities they considered that the Faculty of Divinity was very inadequately equipped and agreed with those authorities who claimed that the number of professors and lecturers should be greatly increased. Unfortunately, however, their hands were tied and they were unable to devote any part of the parliamentary grant to this purpose: all they could do, therefore, was to give formal sanction to existing practice by recognizing the degree of B.D. in a general ordinance on the terms on which it was already granted in the various universities. At Edinburgh the commissioners also instituted a separate Faculty of Music, since it was the only university which provided instruction in that department, and permitted the degrees of Mus.B. and Mus.D. to be conferred—the latter *honoris causa tantum* in certain cases.

A major improvement introduced by the commissioners was a much needed increase in the teaching power of the universities by the admission of lecturers and assistants on a proper footing. Lecturers had previously been seldom officially recognized at all, and although perfunctory arrangements had been made for the employment of assistants they were generally remunerated out of the class fees collected by the professor and were thus appointed or dismissed by him more or less at pleasure. The commissioners rectified this state of affairs by empowering the University Courts to appoint lecturers in subjects not already taught within the university, e.g. modern languages, and also in subjects already taught where either specialization or pressure of numbers made such a step desirable. The status of assistants was also improved by making them definite officers of the university, though still appointed on the nomination of the professor; they were to be remunerated out of university funds and could be dismissed only at the instance of the University Court. The only change made in the patronage of professorships was at St. Andrews, where the commissioners transferred the right of nomination to the chairs of humanity, natural history and chemistry from private individuals to the University Court.

On the financial side the commissioners instituted a fee fund in which fees were pooled for the common benefit of the university, and thereby abolished the former undesirable practice by which professors had simply collected the fees paid by the students they taught. The commissioners were not long in discovering that the annual grant of £42,000 was insufficient to meet even the most modest requirements, since, for one thing, responsibility for professors' pensions had been transferred to the University Courts from the Treasury, which had previously been responsible. Consequently, an additional annual grant of £30,000 was allocated to the universities out of the money released by the 'Equivalent Grant' made over by the Education and Local Taxation Account (Scotland) Act of 1892. Even so, the commissioners regretted their lack of funds for encouraging the expansion of the universities by the creation of new professorships, particularly as so large a proportion of the limited funds available had been swallowed up by the endowment of the five chairs of clinical medicine required for the setting up of the conjoint medical school in Dundee.

They had scarcely completed their labours, however, when an unexpected windfall came the way of the Scottish universities. In June 1901 Mr. Andrew Carnegie, the American millionaire of Scottish birth, presented a sum of £2,000,000 for the encouragement of university education in Scotland. A special Trust was set up to look after this money, which was to be devoted equally to the expansion of the universities and to paying the fees of deserving students of Scottish parentage. Under the first head the expansion might take the form of new lectureships, fellowships and scholarships for special research, or grants in aid of publication of works of learning unlikely to be a commercial proposition. This expansion was restricted mainly to the Faculties of Science and Medicine, and to the more 'modern' subjects in Arts, such as English, modern languages, history and economics, but it has proved of enormous assistance in supplementing the slender finances of the Scottish universities.

About the same time their position was eased in certain other ways as well. The Education Act of 1908, for instance, permitted the Secretary for Scotland to increase the universities' share of the Equivalent Grant out of the Education (Scotland) Fund, if he saw fit. In 1918 the new education authorities were also permitted to extend a limited assistance to the universities out of the school fund, though none of them took advantage of this; in England, on the other hand, local authorities have frequently made grants to the newer universities. But the main source of increased prosperity has been the greatly extended scale of government grants following upon the establishment of the University Grants Committee in 1919. This committee consists of a body of experts in university administration who voluntarily give their services in advising the Treasury on the needs of university education in Great Britain as a whole. The grants recommended may be either recurrent or non-recurrent, and there are no longer any irksome restrictions on the total amount that may be spent, although in recent years there has been some misgiving about the lack of public control over the large sums now annually voted for university education.

The important developments which have taken place in the sphere of applied science have added subjects such as forestry, mining, veterinary science and technical chemistry to the original list. In Medicine there has been a move to undertake the professional training of dental surgeons, and some of the universities have endeavoured to link up with the business world by providing a degree in Commerce (B. Com.). Under the powers of affiliation granted by the act of 1889 the University of Glasgow has affiliated the Royal Technical College for certain purposes, and the University of Edinburgh has taken similar action in regard to the Heriot-Watt College and the Royal (Dick) Veterinary College.

By a joint ordinance of all the Scottish universities a Scottish Universities Entrance Board, situated at St. Andrews, was set up in 1918 to determine from time to time minimum conditions of entry and to scrutinize and decide upon the various leaving and school certificates submitted for the Board's consideration. At the close of the First World War all the Scottish universities, in common with other British universities, instituted the junior doctorate of Ph.D., the requirements for which were less exacting than those demanded for the higher degrees previously established by the commissioners under the act of 1889. The institution of this degree necessitated the abolition of the former degree of D.Phil., candidates for which were henceforth to receive the degree of D.Litt. instead. The new degree might be taken in any Faculty on completion of a thesis prepared under supervision, and although susceptible of abuse it has on the whole done something to stimulate post-graduate research, a field in which the Scottish universities have been conspicuously weak.

The power of framing new ordinances conferred upon the University Courts by virtue of section 21 of the act of 1889 (their power having previously been limited to making changes in existing ordinances) has obviated the necessity for major legislation since that time. It has been found that most matters can be dealt with by ordinance, but there have been two minor pieces of legislation which may be briefly mentioned. The considerable increase in the non-professorial staff has necessitated a greater degree of recognition of the part they play in the affairs of the university, though even yet they cannot be said to have adequate representation on university committees. By an act passed on 20th July 1922 the University Courts were empowered to admit a proportion of readers and lecturers to the Senatus Academicus, and the privilege of membership of the General Council was extended to all lecturers after one year's service, though without the right of voting in a parliamentary election.[1] By the same act the University Courts were authorized to introduce compulsory retiring ages for principals and professors and to adopt, in lieu of their former pensions scheme, the more flexible federated superannuation system for universities.

The other parliamentary measure resulted from the union of the United Free Church with the Church of Scotland on 2nd October 1929, nearly ninety years after the Disruption, and rectified in some degree the deficiencies in the Divinity Faculties complained of by the Scottish Universities Commissioners. The former United Free Church had maintained well-equipped theological colleges

[1] By the Representation of the People Act of 1918 parliamentary representation of the Scottish universities had been increased to three members for a combined constituency of the four universities, but subsequently all university constituencies were abolished by the Representation of the People Act of 1948.

in Edinburgh, Glasgow and Aberdeen, and an act of 16th June 1932 permitted the universities to increase the teaching power of their theological Faculties by absorbing such of these chairs as they deemed desirable. The patronage of all Regius chairs in theology was surrendered to the relative University Court, and the principle of joint consultation between the University Courts and the Church of Scotland over future theological appointments was introduced. A board of nomination composed of equal numbers of representatives of the University Court and the General Assembly of the Church of Scotland was to be set up at each university, and the Church was required to guarantee the salaries of the holders of former Church chairs. In the individual agreements reached between the General Assembly and the University Courts it was also stipulated that all such holders must be ordinands of the Church of Scotland. In this way the teaching power of most of the theological Faculties was practically doubled, and though no United Free Church college had previously existed at St. Andrews it was even found practicable to increase the staff of St. Mary's College there by establishing two additional chairs in theology.

PART V

THE TWENTIETH CENTURY

CHAPTER XI

THE LEGISLATION OF 1908 AND 1918

It was generally expected that the English Education Act of 1902, by which school boards were replaced as the local education authority by County and County Borough Councils, would be followed by a parallel measure for Scotland, but in spite of a number of attempts nothing was actually effected for several years afterwards. In the meantime, however, some progress was made towards meeting the needs of handicapped children in the Education of Defective Children (Scotland) Act of 1906. This was a point to which some attention had already been paid in previous legislation, for in section 69 of the act of 1872 the provision regarding attendance had been specifically declared to include blind children. By the Blind and Deaf-Mute Children (Scotland) Act of 1890 deaf children over seven were likewise included, and school boards were authorized to make special educational provision for both blind and deaf children up to the age of sixteen. The act of 1906 was more comprehensive and extended the same facilities to epileptic, crippled and mentally or physically handicapped children incapable of receiving proper benefit from the instruction in ordinary schools.

Eventually, in 1908, a full-scale Education Act was passed, but the Scottish parochial tradition of two hundred years proved more resistant than its counterpart in England which had lasted only thirty. In consequence, the parish continued as the educational administrative area for most purposes, and school boards were retained, but their powers were considerably extended. Recognition of the county as the more convenient area for secondary education, and the province for the training of teachers, was, however, implicit in the act, which gave statutory sanction to the secondary education committees and the four provincial committees for the training of teachers already established by minutes of the Department. The chief additional powers conferred on the school boards enabled them to incur expenditure, and defray it out of the school fund, for a variety of purposes not hitherto authorized and including the physical, as well as the spiritual, well-being of the children. They might now provide any form of education sanctioned by code or minute of the Department, supply school meals exclusive of the actual cost of the food, pay travelling or maintenance expenses for children from outlying parts of their district, establish an agency for giving vocational guidance to children leaving school, and provide free school books and stationery where required. They were also authorized to institute medical inspection and supervision for children attending school in their district, and where special provision for the education of defective children under the act of 1906 had been made they might make attendance compulsory for such children up to sixteen years of age.

The act did not extend the leaving age in the case of normal children, but it amended previous legislation to some extent. The duty of parents was defined as that of providing 'efficient education', and not merely efficient elementary education in reading, writing and arithmetic, for their children between five and fourteen years of age. For the sake of convenience school boards were permitted, with the Department's approval, to prescribe certain specific dates for commencing and terminating attendance at school, and pupils were bound to remain at school until the next prescribed date after attaining the age of fourteen.

The power of issuing attendance orders, previously vested in the sheriff by the act of 1883, was now transferred to the school boards themselves, thus greatly strengthening their hold over negligent parents. Exemption, although abolished by the act of 1901 for mere proficiency in examination, might still be granted to children of twelve for compassionate or other reasons, and the new act empowered the boards to make such exemption, between twelve and fourteen, conditional on part-time attendance at continuation classes up to sixteen years of age, if they saw fit.

The duty of providing further instruction in the form of continuation classes for all young people above fourteen was also laid on school boards, and they were given permissive powers of enforcing attendance at them up to seventeen years of age in the case of those not otherwise receiving a suitable education. The course of instruction was to have reference to the crafts and industries practised in the district and must further include English language and literature, the laws of health, and opportunity for suitable physical training. In Gaelic-speaking districts the school board might add Gaelic language and literature.

The power of school boards in the matter of granting pensions to their employees was also greatly extended, and similar powers were likewise conferred on the governing bodies of endowed schools, central institutions and the provincial committees. So far as elementary teachers alone were concerned, Scotland had been included in the Elementary School Teachers (Superannuation) Act of 1898, but this was to be superseded by a scheme applicable to all teachers employed by any of the foregoing bodies. The scheme was to be on a contributory basis, and the Department was authorized to deduct 6% of the teachers' salaries from any grants payable to school boards and managers of schools. The latter might in turn recover up to 4% from the teachers to whom the scheme applied, but the remaining 2% had to be found out of the school fund or endowment concerned. The Department was directed to take actuarial advice and prepare a regular superannuation scheme as soon as possible after the passing of the act. The scheme remained in force until 1919, when the introduction of a non-contributory scheme for teachers in England necessitated a revision of its terms. The Education (Scotland) (Superannuation) Act of that year made superannuation in Scotland also non-contributory, but this concession was short-lived. As a result of the so-called 'Geddes Axe' an amending act was passed in 1922 requiring an immediate contribution of 5% from the teachers and authorizing a further 2% from their employers as from 16th May 1923. Finally, after further discussion by Departmental Committees in both countries, the position was stabilized in 1925 by equalizing the contributions of both parties at 5%.

One of the greatest services rendered to Scottish education by the act was the simplification of finance. Under section 15 a central pool, to be known as the Education (Scotland) Fund, was to be instituted, and all the miscellaneous sums payable out of the Local Taxation (Scotland) Account, as well as the general aid grant, were to be paid into it yearly for distribution by the Department. These included the Residue Grant, the Equivalent Grant as applicable to secondary education, and the Secondary and Technical Education Grant of 1898, which, with the general aid grant, amounted to about half-a-million pounds annually. Certain first charges on this money were specified in the act, and comprised the following purposes: providing for the expense of inspecting and examining intermediate and secondary schools and conducting the Leaving Certificate examination; making payments towards the expenditure of universities, central institutions and provincial committees; subsidizing teachers' superannuation; and providing for any other educational expenditure approved by the Department with parliamentary sanction.

After all claims from any of these quarters had been met, the balance of the fund was to be distributed among the secondary education committees for the promotion of education within their districts. They were to be given wide discretion in the application of their share of the money, but the act laid down a number of definite uses to which the funds available should primarily be put. These were payments to school boards on behalf of children from outside the board district who were in attendance at an intermediate or secondary school maintained by the board; payments to the governing bodies of endowed schools for the same purpose, or to any such school considered in need of assistance in the committee's district; establishing a district bursary scheme to enable duly qualified pupils to attend intermediate or secondary schools, technical colleges, central institutions, universities or training centres; meeting one-half of the cost of the medical inspection and supervision of pupils provided by any school board in accordance with section 4 of the act; payment of salaries and expenses of teachers of specialist subjects employed by a committee to supplement the staff of any school or schools in their district; meeting one-half of the capital expenditure on educational provision for defective children, or on workshops or laboratories required by specialist teachers employed by either the committee itself or any school board in its district; and, finally, promoting any educational purpose that might appear to the Department incidental to the district generally rather than to any particular school board. If, after all this, any balance should still remain, it was to be distributed among the school boards and managers of other elementary schools, as an addition to the fee-grant, in compensation for the loss of the general aid grant they had formerly enjoyed. Both secondary education committees and school boards managing an intermediate or secondary school were authorized to establish and maintain, with the consent of the Department, hostels for pupils in attendance at such schools.

In section 21 the right of appeal to the Department was given to any teacher dismissed by a school board. In section 22 school boards were given the option of uniting their districts for all purposes, with the approval of the Department. Previous legislation had permitted the combination of school boards for the provision of schools, and the compulsory union of districts in which there were no public schools. Some advantage seems to have been taken of this clause, for the number of districts decreased from 967 in 1911 to 947 in 1918. In section 26 the duties and powers of school boards in relation to higher class public schools under their management were greatly extended, and in section 27 the limitation of the number of members of a board to a maximum of fifteen was removed. The governing bodies of endowed intermediate or secondary schools were permitted to transfer such schools to the school board of the parish or burgh in which the school was situated, and the relative board was authorized by section 29 to accept the transfer.

In cases where the yearly revenue, being less than £1,000 per annum, was insufficient to maintain the school in a condition of efficiency as a place of higher education, the Department was empowered to compel its transfer if the school board were willing to undertake the duty. But the direct management of any schools transferred under this section must be entrusted to a special committee appointed by the school board and constituted in accordance with the Department's approval. In section 30 endowments applicable to granting bursaries or paying school fees must in future be awarded in conformity with the district education scheme if producing under £1,000 annual revenue. Between £50 and £1,000 the administration was to be left in the hands of the existing governing bodies, but in cases where the revenue was less than £50 it was to be paid over to the secondary education committee for distribution by them. The power of the Department to vary the district or alter the constitution of a secondary education committee was safeguarded by section 31, and the second of these powers was shortly afterwards taken advantage of in view of the new responsibilities devolving on these committees. This was a further step towards making the county the unit of educational administration in Scotland.

Another measure passed in the same session is of interest from the educational point of view, in so far as it dealt with industrial and reformatory schools. This was the Children Act of 1908 which codified the previous legislation designed to make provision for the training, clothing and feeding of neglected children. Though the nomenclature was not rigidly fixed, industrial schools generally catered for vagrant children, while reformatory schools aimed at reforming delinquent boys and girls. In the first instance both types of institution began under voluntary effort, but state action soon followed.

The first Industrial Schools (Scotland) Act was passed in 1854 and was followed by a similar measure for England and Wales in 1857. Children between seven and fourteen, convicted of vagrancy, might be committed to a school certified by the Committee of Council on Education, but in 1860 such schools were transferred to the Home Secretary. Various amendments were made and in 1866 the Industrial Schools Act consolidated the legislation for both countries, allowing detention of destitute children (with or without conviction) up to the age of sixteen. The Elementary Education Act of 1876 had introduced into England the day industrial school, which neglected children could be compelled to attend daily to receive elementary education, industrial training and one or more meals, without being obliged to live in. The Parker Committee advocated the extension of this system to Scotland in 1888, and in 1893 a Day Industrial Schools (Scotland) Act was passed for the establishment of such schools. Apart, however, from Glasgow, which had had special powers in this connection since 1878, only one day industrial school was actually opened, in Edinburgh, in 1898.

The first act dealing with reformatory schools was also passed in 1854, namely the Youthful Offenders Act, but it applied to the United Kingdom as a whole. It empowered the Home Secretary to certify reformatory schools, and permitted offenders under sixteen to be sent to them, on the expiration of their prison sentence, for a period of between two and five years. Again minor adjustments were subsequently made and, as in the case of industrial schools, consolidating legislation was introduced, in 1866, by the Reformatory Schools Act. In 1893 the Reformatory Schools (Scotland) Act introduced a principle which was adopted in the same year for Great Britain, that of dispensing with previous imprisonment as a necessary condition for sending a child to a reformatory, and in 1899 another Reformatory Schools Act definitely abolished the previous imprisonment, which was the chief distinction between reformatory and industrial schools.

Since there remained principally the difference in age, although in fact there was also the moral distinction between being an offender oneself and having the misfortune to come of negligent parents, it was suggested that both types of school should be classified on the same basis, as Senior and Junior Home Office Schools. In 1896 a Departmental Committee under Sir Godfrey Lushington had also recommended that both classes of school should be placed under the control of the Secretary for Scotland. Accordingly, in the act of 1908 industrial and reformatory schools were dealt with together, the former being defined as a school for the industrial training of children under fourteen, in which they were lodged, clothed and fed, as well as taught, and the latter as a school of a similar nature for the industrial training of youthful offenders between fourteen and sixteen. At the same time the principal provisions regarding day industrial schools were re-enacted, and the Secretary for Scotland was substituted for the Home Secretary in respect of industrial and reformatory schools in Scotland. Thus the position remained until 1932, except that by section 19 of the Education (Scotland) Act of 1918 the Secretary for Scotland might transfer to the Department any powers conferred upon him in connection with these schools under the act of 1908.

It was only to be expected that the social upheaval caused by the First World War should lead to profound changes in the educational system of the country, and in 1918 education acts were passed for both England and Scotland. The Scottish measure received the royal assent on 21st November 1918, and at length the county replaced the parish as the unit of educational administration. The local authority for education was not yet, however, the County or County Borough Council acting through a special education committee, as it had been in England since 1902, but an *ad hoc* authority elected triennially, more or less like a school board, save that the novel principle of proportional representation was introduced at any contested election. The act enumerated in all thirty-eight of these education authorities, one for each county and one for the 'scheduled burghs' of Edinburgh, Glasgow, Aberdeen, Dundee and Leith. The determination of the electoral divisions within each area and the number of members for each authority was left at the discretion of the Secretary for Scotland, but he was instructed to have regard to existing wards in the scheduled burghs, and to parishes, districts and other burghs in the case of counties.

As a concession to local opinion every authority was required to submit for the approval of the Department a scheme of school management committees (or area sub-committees) for the management of schools or groups of schools under their control throughout the area. The constitution of these committees was to include due representation of the authority itself and of the parents of children attending the schools, at least one teacher engaged in the schools on the nomination of his colleagues, and in the case of a committee managing a transferred voluntary school a representative of the relative denomination. In counties it was proposed that separate committees should probably be constituted for individual burghs and parishes. These committees might exercise all the powers and duties of the authority itself in regard to the general management of the schools (including attendance), subject, however, to any restrictions imposed by the education authority; but where a secondary school was concerned no restrictions might be imposed. The act stipulated, on the other hand, that the power of levying a rate, acquiring land, appointing and dismissing teachers and granting bursaries, and of recognizing or discontinuing secondary schools, must in all cases be exercised only by the authority.

The powers and duties of education authorities were defined in sections 4 to 13 of the act. In many cases these resembled those performed by the secondary education committees under the act of 1908, but there were important differences. The school fund, for instance, might now be used instead of the district education fund, which had not been rate-aided, for assisting qualified pupils to attend intermediate or secondary schools, universities, training colleges or central institutions. In the counties the provision of free books, by virtue of an arrangement made with the county library, might be extended to adults as an ancillary means of promoting education. Every authority, while retaining the right to maintain in addition a limited number of fee-paying schools, must now make adequate provision of free primary, intermediate and secondary education (including the teaching of Gaelic, where applicable) throughout its area. Where previously school boards had made their own arrangements with the teachers they employed, the new education authorities were required to institute a scale of salaries in accordance with a minimum national scale laid down by the Department. The permissive powers of education authorities to continue the custom of providing religious instruction, subject to a conscience clause, were made explicit by incorporating in section 7 the relevant excerpt from the preamble of the act of 1872.

The education authorities were also granted permissive powers not only to establish nursery schools for children between two and five, but also to look after the health, nourishment and physical welfare of the children in attendance. They might contribute to the maintenance of voluntary or endowed schools included within their scheme of educational provision for the area (on condition that the teachers employed were paid at the same rate as corresponding teachers in their own service), and make grants to central institutions and universities. But, in the case of schools and central institutions, they might make any such contribution conditional upon reasonable representation on the governing body. This condition did not, however, apply to independent intermediate or secondary schools previously in receipt of payments out of the district education fund under the act of 1908, and all authorities were compelled to continue these contributions at a level not lower than that in force at 15th May 1914. A new obligation imposed on the local authorities was the payment of contributions towards the expense of training colleges in each year, in proportion to the number of fully qualified teachers in their employment. Finally, with the sanction of the Department, any education authority might contribute to the maintenance of any educational institution or agency considered likely to be of benefit to persons resident within its area—the term 'persons' implying, in particular, the promotion of adult education.

Sections 14 to 17 dealt with the extension of the school leaving age, continuation classes and the employment of children. On a day to be appointed the school age was to be extended to fifteen and exemption restricted to children over thirteen years of age. The fixing of the appointed day for the raising of the age was left at the discretion of the Department, doubtless so that policy in the matter might be co-ordinated with the situation in England, but for a variety of reasons the discretion was never exercised. Eventually it was fixed by statute as 1st September 1939, but the outbreak of the Second World War caused it to be postponed. Some improvement was, however, effected by compelling the new authorities to exercise their powers of prescribing dates of commencing and terminating school attendance under section 7 of the act of 1908.

Every authority was also required to submit for the Department's approval a scheme of continuation classes, in the first instance for young persons under sixteen, and, when required, for those between sixteen and eighteen. Again it was intended to make attendance at these classes compulsory for all who left school at the minimum age—up to sixteen within one year of the appointed day and eventually up to eighteen—but this provision was likewise never put into effect. The local authorities were empowered to require continued attendance for any time up to three months beyond the date on which the requisite age had been attained. It was laid down that the scheme should provide for instruction in English language and literature and in such other parts of a general education as might be desirable, for vocational education in present or prospective employment and for physical education adapted to age and physique. The minimum attendance required was to be an aggregate total of not less than 320 hours per annum and the instruction must be provided between the hours of 8 a.m. and 7 p.m. The obligation of attendance up to eighteen was, however, not to be enforced until three years after the institution of compulsory attendance up to the age of sixteen, and responsibility for regular attendance was, for the first time under any education act, placed upon the young person himself and not on his parents. Certain restrictions in the employment of children outside school hours and in specific occupations were also laid down: after the appointed day no child under thirteen was to be employed before 8 a.m. or after 6 p.m., nor was any child under fifteen to be employed in a factory, coal mine or quarry, to which certain specified acts were applicable.

A very important section of the act dealt with voluntary or denominational schools, which, although grant-aided, were not under public control. Any voluntary school within the meaning of the Education (Scotland) Act of 1897, in terms of which state-aid to such schools had previously been regulated, might be transferred to the appropriate education authority by sale, lease or other agreement, and the latter was bound to accept the transfer and maintain the school thereafter as a public school. An element of compulsion was introduced by discontinuing all public grants to any non-transferred school after the expiry of two years from the passing of the act, with the exception of a number of residential orphanages and establishments for defective children, the inmates of which might be drawn from wider areas.

To ease the transfer of these schools reasonable concessions were made to the denominations affected. The existing staffs were to be taken over and put on the authority's salary scale at the appropriate point, and while new appointments were required to satisfy the regulations of the Department as to academic qualifications, the denominations retained the right of approving such teachers as regards their religious beliefs. The time set apart for religious instruction and observance in transferred schools must be not less than formerly and the authority was bound to grant facilities for the appointment by the denomination of an unpaid supervisor to ensure that the religious instruction was being efficiently carried on.

In this straightforward way the so-called 'religious question', apparently so complex in English education, was finally resolved in Scotland. To meet future needs, any voluntary school that might be established could, with the consent of the Department, be similarly transferred, or alternatively an education authority itself might, on satisfying the Department of the need, establish a denominational school of its own. Should the need for a denominational school cease to exist, the authority might apply to the Department, at any time after the expiry of ten years from the transfer or provision of such a school, for sanction either to discontinue it or to transform it into an ordinary public school. In the case of a transferred school, compensation might be payable to the original trustees in either of these events.

For the purpose of advising the Department on educational matters the act provided for the establishment by order in council of an Advisory Council on Education in Scotland. The membership of this body was to consist, up to not less than two-thirds of the total, of persons qualified to represent the views of various bodies interested in education, and the Department was directed to take into consideration any advice or representation submitted to it by the Advisory Council. The powers thus conferred were considerably more extensive than those enjoyed by the Consultative Committee to the Board of Education in England, established in 1900, for the latter might advise only on matters referred to it by the Board, and not on its own initiative. Even so, however, it was a number of years before the Advisory Council succeeded in making its influence greatly felt in Scottish educational affairs.

The financial basis of Scottish education was also radically reorganized as a result of the act, and the functions of the Education (Scotland) Fund were extended to include the distribution of all monies voted by Parliament for education in Scotland. In addition to the various sums payable out of the Local Taxation (Scotland) Account under section 15 of the act of 1908, a standard grant equal to the actual expenditure incurred during the fiscal year 1913-14 was to be paid into the Fund, and annual adjustments were to be made on the basis of eleven-eightieths of any estimated excess over the corresponding standard grant for England and Wales in successive years. The standard grant was thus fixed at some £2,300,000, and expenditure was largely stabilized to allow of more accurate budgeting, but one somewhat serious inconvenience introduced by the new arrangement was that the annual adjustment was based upon an estimated increase in expenditure in England and Wales. If, therefore, the actual expenditure were to exceed or fall short of this amount, the Education (Scotland) Fund would suffer a proportionate increase or reduction in the following year. The first charges enumerated in the act of 1908 were still to be met, and the balance was to be applied in making grants in aid of the expenditure of education authorities and managers of endowed schools.

The remaining provisions of the act can be discussed quite briefly. Teachers' security of tenure was safeguarded, education authorities were required to establish in their area a local advisory council to advise them on matters of educational interest, and women were not to be precluded either by sex or by marriage from membership of any of the statutory bodies relating to education. A more significant innovation was the alteration of the

Department's official designation to the 'Scottish Education Department' by section 30 of the act, an improvement which had long been desired by Scottish opinion. This change of name heralded also a greater degree of devolution in Scottish educational administration. For some time the Department had maintained an office in Edinburgh, but the first two secretaries, Sir Henry Craik, Bart., and Sir John Struthers, established their headquarters at the Scottish Office in Dover House, Whitehall. Soon after the appointment of Sir George Macdonald in 1922, however, the Department began to operate more and more from Edinburgh, although the transfer was not finally completed until 1939. Lastly, by section 33, the appointed day for bringing the various provisions of the act into operation was left largely to the discretion of the Department, and different days for different purposes were expressly sanctioned. The financial provisions, however, were in any case to come into operation on 1st April 1919, and by a departmental order of 20th February the date of the first election of the *ad hoc* education authorities was fixed for 24th February 1919. Apart from the clauses raising the school age and instituting compulsory continuation classes, most of the remaining provisions came into force on 16th May 1919.

The *ad hoc* education authorities served to consolidate the county and large burgh as the unit of administration in place of the parish, but otherwise they were short-lived. By 1920 their number had already been reduced to thirty-seven by the amalgamation of Leith with Edinburgh, and by the Local Government (Scotland) Act of 1929 the system was brought into alignment with that which had been in operation in England since 1902. In section 3 of the act the Town Council of a burgh being a county of a city[1], and the County Council of a county, was constituted the education authority for the purposes of the Education

[1] The Scottish equivalent of the English county borough.

(Scotland) Acts. In section 10 the combination of the County Councils of Perth and Kinross and of Moray and Nairn to form joint County Councils reduced the number of county authorities from thirty-three to thirty-one, which with the four Town Councils of the scheduled burghs stabilized the number of education authorities at thirty-five. By section 12 each County Council and Town Council of a scheduled burgh was directed to constitute a committee, to be known as the Education Committee, and to refer to that committee all matters relating to education, except those relating to the raising of money by rate or loan, before exercising its functions in regard to educational questions. In this connection any decision regarding the provision of religious instruction under section 7 of the Education Act of 1918 was expressly mentioned. The precise composition of Education Committees was not stated, but it was laid down that they must comprise at least a majority of members of the relative Town or County Council, and for the rest persons of experience in education or acquainted with the needs of the various kinds of school in the area, at least two persons interested in the promotion of religious instruction under the permissive clause of the 1918 act, and at least one representative of any denominational school transferred to the authority and managed under section 18 of that act.

The Local Government (Scotland) Act also introduced a slight readjustment into educational finance by standardizing the amount previously paid into the Education (Scotland) Fund from the Local Taxation (Scotland) Account. By section 52 the Account was to be wound up as soon as possible after 31st March 1930, and in the sixth schedule Parliament agreed to vote annually a sum equal in amount to the payments made from it in the financial year ending on 31st March 1929. At the same time the annual sum of £30,000, to be paid to the Scottish Universities under the original act of 1892, was guaranteed to them. In conclusion, another piece of legislation, though not directly affecting education, may be mentioned as enhancing the importance of purely Scottish affairs at that time. This was the Secretaries of State Act of 1926, by which the powers and duties of the Secretary for Scotland were to become the powers and duties of a principal Secretary of State, whose number was increased to a total of six for the purpose. So far as Scottish education was concerned, this meant that the responsible minister, henceforth the Secretary of State for Scotland, was assured *ex officio* of a seat in the Cabinet of the Government of the day.

CHAPTER XII

TEACHER TRAINING SINCE 1906

THE establishment in 1905 of regional committees for the training of teachers was a major revolution in the administrative system of education in Scotland. From 1906 these committees took over the work of the former university local committees, and in 1907 they formally assumed responsibility for the management of the six church training colleges in the cities of Edinburgh, Glasgow and Aberdeen. They acted independently of each other and were financed by a direct grant from the Department to cover the cost of training and maintenance allowances made to students, but the four committees pursued a common policy of co-ordinating the facilities within their area. In the three large university cities the unnecessary duplication of effort was abolished by a process of amalgamation, and the double training colleges were reduced in each instance to a single training centre catering for all grades of teacher.

The training facilities at St. Andrews and Dundee were also put on a more satisfactory basis, although there the problem was slightly different since it involved the co-ordination of two King's Student Centres but no college for non-university candidates. To supply this want it was proposed to establish an ordinary training college in Dundee on the model of the unitary provincial colleges in other centres, but in the case of graduate students a certain amount of training was still to be carried on at St. Andrews under the auspices of the committee. Mr. J. S. Malloch, Lecturer in Education at Dundee University College, was appointed Director of Studies to the St. Andrews Provincial Committee, and the Dundee Department of Education was placed under the chair at St. Andrews. Since no suitable building was available, the nucleus of the future training college was housed in temporary premises within the grounds of the University College in the former Technical Institute. The arrangement lasted longer than had been anticipated, for although a new building was begun in Park Place in 1912, the outbreak of war in 1914 held up completion until 1920.

The Department also introduced far-reaching changes in the actual system of training by requiring that in future not only teachers in primary schools but also those in secondary schools and teachers of special subjects such as art, handwork, music, rural economy, domestic science and the like should receive an adequate preparation for their work. By the 'Regulations for the preliminary Education, Training, and Certification of Teachers for various Grades of Schools' which came into operation in July 1906 no less than three types of certificate were recognized. The qualification for teaching in primary schools was the Teacher's General Certificate, awarded after a two years' training college course or a one year's post-graduate course at a training college; that for teaching a higher subject in a secondary school was the Teacher's Special Certificate, awarded to candidates with an honours degree in Arts or Science, after a course of professional training approved by the Department; and that for teaching a so-called 'technical' subject in any grant-earning school was the not very happily named Teacher's Technical Certificate, awarded to candidates with a diploma of an institution recognized for the purpose, after an approved course of professional training.[1] Recognition was with-

[1] The three types of training were at first designated by the relative chapter numbers of the Regulations and the actual names were not specified till later.

drawn from post-graduate university diplomas, and even the new certificates were merely provisional, since two years' satisfactory service in a school approved by the Department was required before they were made permanent.

The pupil-teacher system was also done away with after sixty years, and replaced by a more satisfactory 'junior student system' which at least ensured a sounder secondary education among prospective teachers. Centres for these 'junior students' were established in higher grade or secondary schools and as a condition of acceptance every candidate was required to have passed the Intermediate Certificate. Thereafter there followed a three years' course of combined professional training and general education up to the age of 18, along similar lines to the old pupil-teacher system but on a higher level of attainment. The Department prescribed a curriculum comprising English, history, geography, a foreign language, mathematics, science, art, music and physical training, and expected all candidates to take the Leaving Certificate examination in some of these subjects. Successful candidates were awarded the Junior Student Certificate and might proceed as a 'senior student' to a recognized training college. It was objected to the new system, however, that the combination of advanced academic work with practical teaching overworked the students, and further that the very variety of subjects in the prescribed curriculum necessitated a degree of segregation at an early age from those pursuing a normal (and more specialized) course of secondary education. Finally, all uncertificated teachers were required by the new regulations to undergo training by the end of 1914, after which provisional recognition by the Department would expire.

The practical effect of these changes was at one and the same time to concentrate teacher-training around the four universities and yet to diminish their share in the professional training of teachers. The university courses in education, it is true, might still be taken as qualifying courses for the M.A. degree, but the universities were desirous of taking a more active part. Accordingly, the University of Edinburgh instituted a new Diploma in Education which might be taken concurrently with a year's post-graduate training under a provincial committee, in lieu of the professional instruction in education and psychology provided at the training centre. A second-year course leading to the full degree of Bachelor of Education was added in 1917, and similar action was taken by the other three Scottish universities. In course of time many of the more promising graduate students in training have come to prefer the combined course, leading to the university diploma in addition to the Department's certificate. A fair number of these have later gone on, either immediately or after a spell of practical experience, to complete the degree, which is now widely recognized as the passport to posts of responsibility in specialist branches of the educational service.

The relationship between the universities and the training centres was strengthened by the subsequent linking of the two Bell chairs of education with the posts of Director of Studies to the Edinburgh[1] and St. Andrews Provincial Committees. This was accomplished in 1925 and has contributed greatly to raising the professional part of the teacher's training to a university level. No such formal link exists at Glasgow or Aberdeen, but cordial relations have always subsisted between the university department and the provincial training college. Indeed at Aberdeen, for a considerable number of years, the same staff of lecturers in both education and psychology conducted the courses jointly for each institution. One somewhat regrettable feature of the expansion of education as

[1] The position in Edinburgh was modified on the retirement of Sir Godfrey Thomson from the joint appointment in September 1951.

a university subject has been its removal from the ordinary graduation course in Arts, where it was regarded by many as a study of great cultural and educational value. As has been rightly said, 'The study of education is itself an education'.

The Education (Scotland) Act of 1918 brought further changes in the existing system of teacher training. Under the act the new education authorities, which replaced the former school boards, were bound to make a contribution to the cost of training in their area, proportional to the number of qualified teachers they employed. In consequence, the Scottish Education Department took the view that this duty implied a measure of control over the expenditure involved in the training of teachers. As a result, the existing autonomous provincial committees were reconstituted by a minute of 10th February 1920 and a new co-ordinating National Committee for the Training of Teachers was established.

In the meantime, the facilities for training had been increased by the opening of a second residential Roman Catholic college for women at Moray Place, Edinburgh, in 1919,[1] and also by the founding of a residential College of Hygiene and Physical Education for women at Dunfermline, by the Carnegie Dunfermline Trust. Arrangements were made whereby all the remaining training agencies should come under the ultimate control of the new National Committee, but with the exception of the training department at St. George's School in Edinburgh, which was placed under the Edinburgh Provincial Committee, special committees of management were authorized for those centres. They comprised the Episcopal and Roman Catholic colleges in Edinburgh, the Roman Catholic college in Glasgow and the Physical Education College at Dunfermline, all of them residential women's colleges. The Edinburgh Episcopal college did not, however, long

[1] Subsequently moved to Craiglockhart.

survive the change; dwindling numbers of students forced it to amalgamate with the Edinburgh Provincial College in 1929 for lecture purposes, although it continued to maintain a separate hostel at Dalry House until 1934.

The management of the four principal centres remained as before, in the hands of the Provincial Committees, which were now relieved of financial responsibility. By the new financial arrangements the expenditure of the National Committee was to be met from four main sources: namely, the fees paid by the students, capitation grants per student in training, grants up to 75% of approved capital expenditure from the Education (Scotland) Fund, and contributions from education authorities. The last item is calculated from 31st March and represents the difference between estimated income from other sources and expenditure for the coming year. This residue is divided by the total number of teachers in service on 31st March and levied from the education authorities as a quota per teacher employed. As an example of the percentages of the total received from each of the sources, the income for the academic year 1938-9 was made up of 51% contributions from education authorities, 23% capitation grants, 19% students' fees, 5% grants for capital expenditure and about 2% from minor sources.

In consequence of the amount contributed by the education authorities, the members of the National Committee are all representatives of education authorities and are chosen from among the members of their education committees. Every education authority has at least one member, but authorities employing larger numbers of teachers may have more. These numbers are determined from time to time by minutes of the Department and in 1946 the National Committee consisted of forty-five members. So august a body seldom meets more than once a year, to approve general policy, and the day-to-day business is carried on by a Central Executive Committee representing both the National Committee and other interests. Out of a total membership of twenty-one the National Committee provides eleven—its chairman and ten other members—from among its own number. The remaining ten members are the four chairmen of Provincial Committees, the three chairmen of Committees of Management, two teachers' representatives and one representative of the Church of Scotland Education Committee. The National Committee's office is in Edinburgh and its affairs are looked after by a full-time executive officer.

The Provincial Committees have been somewhat reduced in size as a result of the unification of education authorities following upon the Education (Scotland) Act of 1918, but they are roughly representative of the same interests as before. For instance, the Glasgow Provincial Committee, originally consisting of thirty-eight members exclusive of denominational representatives, has now been reduced to thirty-four, including five representatives of the Education Committee of the Church of Scotland; but the interests represented are still the education authorities in the area, the University Court, the central institutions and practising teachers. In the case of the Provincial Committees the Director of Studies in the training centre acts as executive officer. Finally, the three committees of management consist of ten members in each case: five representing the denomination (or trust), three representing the education authorities and chosen by the relative Provincial Committee, and two representing the National Committee. The Department reserves the right to appoint assessors to serve on all of the foregoing committees.

In 1924 the regulations governing the training of teachers were considerably modified. Perhaps the most important modification was the requirement of graduation from all future male candidates for the Teacher's General Certificate. This was not extended to women, but in their case the junior student system was discontinued and the Leaving Certificate made compulsory for entrance to the training colleges. A certain measure of preliminary training was retained (in subordination to the student's general education) in selected cases, and might even be held equivalent to the first year of a new minimum course of three years. Otherwise, women might graduate like men before taking their training.

The professional requirements for the Teacher's Special and Technical Certificates were laid down in greater detail. For the former a university degree with first or second class honours and a one-year approved course of professional training (including adequate instruction in the administration and organization of schools) was laid down, and for the latter a course of professional training of not less than two terms after the completion of a diploma course at a recognized institution. If taken apart from the general certificate, these certificates qualified their holders for teaching only the subjects specified, but they might be taken in addition to the general certificate with a reduction in the aggregate length of course. Specialist teachers of modern foreign languages were required to spend an academic year in the country where their principal language was spoken and submit, if necessary, to an oral test of proficiency by the Department. Graduates with third class honours were to be admitted only to the general certificate, on the same terms as pass graduates, except that the latter might still take a concurrent degree course in a training college and university (instead of concentrating their training into the post-graduate year). If this alternative were chosen, however, the total length of the combined course was still four years, but it carried the great advantage of offering increased opportunities of teaching practice to those who chose it.

Since these somewhat complicated requirements are enumerated under chapter headings in the regulations, the qualifications conferred under each head are frequently alluded to in that way. Thus, Chapters III and IV deal with the General Certificate, Chapter V with the Special Certificate, and Chapter VI with the Technical Certificate. The new regulations also recognized endorsements of the general and special certificates under certain articles. The most important of these was Article 39, which granted recognition to teach a specified subject in Advanced Division (now Junior Secondary) schools or in the first three years of a full secondary course. Generally speaking, two years' academic study in a university for each subject in which endorsement is desired—and, if in a modern foreign language, three months' residence in the appropriate country and an oral test by the Department—was a preliminary requirement, but non-graduate women were permitted to qualify to teach certain subjects, such as art, commercial subjects, domestic subjects or rural subjects, by taking an extra year's course beyond the General Certificate.

The qualification for teaching physical education was a three-year course at either of the schools of hygiene and physical education, for men at Jordanhill, Glasgow (under the Provincial Committee), and for women at Dunfermline, which led both to the Diploma in Physical Education and to the Technical Certificate, or a one-year course leading to the same qualifications in the case of a holder of either of the other two teacher's certificates. Finally, probation was restricted under Article 49 of the regulations to schools approved for the purpose. The new regulations came into force in 1926 but were again revised in 1931. The course leading to the General Certificate was lengthened to four terms, except in the case of students taking a combined course of university education and professional training. In the case of non-graduating women students all preliminary training concurrent with the Leaving Certificate was abolished and, if taken at all, was thereafter canalized into a post-certificate year in a secondary school. At the same time restrictions on the admission of such students to the normal three years' course in a training college, without preliminary training, were removed.[1] This policy tended perhaps to encourage an increase in the number of non-graduating women teachers but it also discouraged the rather undesirable practice of beginning at the second year of the three year training college course.

Since 1931 the regulations for the training of teachers have remained practically unaltered, except for the emergency training scheme initiated towards the close of the Second World War. No special creation of emergency colleges, as in England, was found necessary in Scotland, and the existing agencies were able to cope with the increased flow of students, although with a certain degree of strain. The scheme did, however, involve relaxation of some of the existing regulations. As far as possible, the principle of graduation for male teachers was retained, but it could not be enforced under all circumstances. By arrangement with the universities, emergency candidates might graduate in two (instead of three) years, and professional training was completed in a further two (instead of four) terms. Otherwise, a course of two years and two terms for men, and two years for women, was prescribed at a recognized training centre in the case of candidates whose previous educational record was insufficient to meet university entrance requirements. The period of probation was also reduced to one year (instead of two) for the benefit of emergency trainees.

Nor have there been any outstanding developments in the administrative system of teacher training in recent years. The departmental committee set up by the Board of Education in England under the chairmanship of Sir

[1] Under the previous regulations women candidates who had not undergone a course of preliminary training while at school were required to graduate before admission to training.

Arnold McNair in March 1942, as a result of which institutes of education were developed in connection with the English universities, did not apply to Scotland. However, in February 1943 the Secretary of State for Scotland remitted certain aspects of the question for the consideration of the Advisory Council on Education, and in November of the same year extended the terms of reference to cover the whole problem of teacher training. That the training of teachers is a national concern, and as such an integral part of the state educational system, was a principle too firmly established in Scotland for there to be any likelihood of its being delegated to the universities. Accordingly, the Advisory Council, in its Report published in January 1946, failed to recommend that responsibility for the training of teachers should be transferred to the universities, but was prepared to advocate the establishment of institutes of education in association with them. Some of the existing centres were considered too large and it was proposed that they should be broken down to form constituent and largely autonomous colleges within each institute. No immediate steps were, however, taken to implement these proposals.

Teachers' terms of service in Scotland as regards salaries and pensions have kept more or less in step with conditions in England but there are certain characteristic features to be noted. Long before the state assumed formal responsibility for an educational service, successive acts of parliament prescribed a minimum national scale of salaries (however inadequate) for parochial schoolmasters. As early as 1807 a measure of superannuation on a contributory basis was established for the relief of widows and orphans of parochial and burgh schoolmasters. Compulsory at first, the scheme was made optional for future contributors by the act of 1861, and discontinued after the passing of the Education (Scotland) Act of 1872. Kay-Shuttleworth's pension system for the teachers themselves, under the minute of 1846, was made applicable to Scotland but was withdrawn under the original Revised Code of 1862, except in the case of teachers already retired. In 1875, however, it was revived for the benefit of former contributors only, and no further general scheme was authorized until 1898, when an Elementary Teachers Superannuation Act, applicable to both England and Scotland, was passed. The Education (Scotland) Act of 1908 authorized the Department to draw up a scheme of superannuation for teachers in all grades of school, whether primary or secondary, public or endowed, and extended its provisions to include those employed by provincial committees and central institutions.

Since then several special superannuation acts have been passed modifying the conditions and bringing them into alignment with those in operation in England. Generally speaking, education authorities, in common with other employers of teachers, are required to pay annually into the Superannuation Scheme for Teachers (Scotland), 1926, a sum equal to 5% of the salaries paid to the teachers in their employment, and the teachers themselves must make an equivalent contribution out of their salaries. On the expiration of their certificates at the age of sixty-five teachers are compelled to retire, but at any time after attaining the age of sixty they may voluntarily resign with a retiring allowance, provided they have fulfilled certain requirements as to previous service. The actual amount of the allowance received is governed by the teacher's average salary over the last five years of his service. It consists of a lump sum not exceeding eighteen months' salary at that rate and an annual pension not exceeding one-half of this 'pensionable' salary. In order to meet these demands the Scheme may be supplemented out of the Education (Scotland) Fund.

By the repeal of earlier legislation on the passing of the Education (Scotland) Act of 1872 the minimum salary scales previously in force were abolished, and the question of teachers' pay was left at the discretion of the individual school boards. This unsatisfactory position remained unchanged until the steep rise in the cost of living during the First World War brought the matter to a head. In 1917 the President of the Board of Education in England appointed a departmental committee to inquire into the principles of constructing salary scales for teachers, and as a result the Burnham Committee, representative of the education authorities and the National Union of Teachers, was constituted two years later under the chairmanship of Lord Burnham. In July 1917 a similar departmental committee was set up for Scotland under Sir Henry Craik, and one of the provisions of the education act of 1918 was that the new education authorities were compelled to institute scales of salary for their teachers in accordance with regulations to be laid down by the Department in consultation with the education authorities and the teaching profession.

Finally, in 1919, negotiations were completed and Minimum National Scales, which remained in force until 31st March 1945, were adopted. These scales, based on the type of certificate held (general, special, or technical) and somewhat lower for women than for men, were minimal, but they might be exceeded. In consequence, there was an inevitable tendency for wealthier authorities and endowed schools to pay slightly higher salaries than were required, in the hope of attracting better qualified teachers. Already in the thirties the disadvantages of fixed scales without adequate negotiating machinery began to be felt, and in January 1939 a National Joint Council was set up to investigate the question of teachers' salaries. Unfortunately the outbreak of war postponed effective action and teachers had to be content with a temporary war bonus to offset the further rise in the cost of living occasioned by the Second World War. However, in 1943 the Advisory Council, in an interim report, recommended the substitution of standard for minimum National Scales. As a result, the National Joint Council was reconstituted in 1944 under the chairmanship of Lord Teviot.

Somewhat analogous to the Burnham Committee, the new Joint Council was to consist of twelve representatives of education authorities, an equal number of teachers' representatives, six assessors representing the Association of Directors of Education and Officers of Local Authorities, and a liaison officer appointed by the Department. In 1945 standard national scales, named after the chairman and subject to revision every three years, came into operation, replacing the former Minimum National Scales. Like their predecessors, and in contradistinction to the revised Burnham Scale adopted in England about the same time, these scales retained the old distinction based on qualification under the various chapters of the regulations instead of accepting the principle of a single basic salary for all qualified teachers, with additional allowances for special qualifications.

Corresponding to the National Union of Teachers in England, the Educational Institute of Scotland supplies the teachers' representatives on the National Joint Council, as well as on the Provincial Committees and the Central Executive Committee. In improving the conditions of service of the teacher and in advancing the cause of education in Scotland generally, this professional body of educationists has done exceedingly valuable work. Founded in 1847 and incorporated by Royal Charter in 1851, the Institute now consists of 26,500 members and publishes weekly *The Scottish Educational Journal*, a periodical which contains a variety of articles on educational questions and current topics of general interest. In addition, it promotes sound learning by maintaining a number of standing committees to deal with questions of curricula, by undertaking publication of smaller works on Scottish education and syllabuses for use in schools, and by subsidizing annually the Scottish Council for Research in Education.

In conclusion, something should be said about the improvement in the teacher's security of tenure which has been achieved since 1872. Under the old dispensation the parochial schoolmaster had held office *ad vitam aut culpam* and could hardly be removed under any circumstances. The acts of 1803 and 1861 did something to mitigate this evil, until the act of 1872 went to the opposite extreme by decreeing that teachers should hold office only during the pleasure of the school board. In view of a number of arbitrary and capricious dismissals following the passing of this act, Mr. A. J. Mundella introduced legislation in 1882 to ensure that no dismissal should take place without due deliberation, or merely by virtue of an accidental majority at a board meeting.

Under the Public Schools (Scotland) Teachers Act of that year no resolution for the dismissal of a certificated teacher might be considered without three weeks' warning to each member of the school board, nor should it be valid unless agreed to by a majority of the full members of the board. A right of appeal to the Department, within six weeks of the adoption of such a resolution, was granted to teachers under section 21 of the act of 1908, with the alternative of compensation amounting up to one year's salary, failing reinstatement, in cases where the resolution was found to be not reasonably justifiable. On the substitution of county education authorities for school boards under the act of 1918, a slight modification of this procedure became necessary. Under section 24 of the act the same amount of notice of a resolution is required and the right of appeal is retained, but in view of the increased numbers involved, only half of the members of the education authority need be present, of whom not less than two thirds must be in favour of the resolution for the dismissal to be valid.

CHAPTER XIII

DEVELOPMENTS BETWEEN 1918 AND 1939

IN THE period between the two World Wars perhaps the most significant ideal which grew up in the public mind was secondary education for all. For the majority of pupils the supplementary courses of 1903, which were held in rather low esteem, were the only provision made, and secondary education proper tended to be excessively academic in conception. Consequently, one of the first tasks which confronted the Department was the reorganization of the system of post-primary education to meet the needs of the post-war world. With characteristic vigour the Department tackled this problem in a circular of December 1921, in which it was proposed to delegate responsibility for conducting the qualifying examination to the new education authorities from 1922 onwards, to discontinue the restricting influence of the Intermediate Certificate and to revise the regulations for the Leaving Certificate to allow greater flexibility in the secondary course as a whole.

The two latter proposals were effected in August 1923 by the introduction of two codes of regulations dealing with the two types of post-primary school: the 'Secondary School (Scotland) Regulations' for distinctively secondary institutions, including the three-year higher grade schools, and the 'Code of Regulations for Day Schools in Scotland' for all other schools. Under the first, the Intermediate Certificate was abolished and the Leaving Certificate examination was broadened by the inclusion of a greater number of alternative subjects, particularly those of a practical nature. The minimum group was reduced to two passes on the higher and two on the lower standard, and no definite subjects, apart from English (including literature and history) on the higher grade, were laid down. The Department continued to expect, however, presentation on at least the lower grade both in mathematics (or science) and in a foreign language as a *sine qua non* for obtaining the certificate, whatever additional subjects might be offered. Under the other code, the supplementary courses were replaced by 'advanced divisions', and the former Intermediate and Merit Certificates were succeeded by two Day School Certificates, higher and lower. Indeed, the whole primary school was reorganized into four divisions—infants (under seven), juniors (seven to nine), seniors (nine to twelve) and an advanced division for those who, about the age of twelve, should have passed the selection examination set by an education authority.

While primarily designed for organization under the Day Schools Code, an advanced division might also be provided under the Secondary School Regulations in certain circumstances. In consequence a variety of types came into existence. As might be expected, the commonest was, like the old supplementary courses, a top to a primary school, but occasionally separate central schools were established for the purpose; again as might be expected, such recognized secondary schools as offered advanced division courses generally provided them running parallel to the secondary course proper, but in a few cases an 'omnibus school' was organized, in which a definite attempt was made to unify and integrate the curriculum of the advanced division with the first three years of the secondary school. A minor difference between the divisions associated with primary schools (or separately organized) and those attached to secondary schools was that in the former two admission dates were generally recognized, to follow the two qualifying examinations normally held annually by every education authority, whereas in the latter admission was necessarily restricted to the beginning of the school year, as for pupils entering the full secondary course.

In three of the largest cities the enrolment in 24 advanced division schools exceeded a thousand pupils, but in the main they tended to be small with an average of under two hundred in attendance. In 1932, 67 out of a total of 251 recognized secondary schools in the country offered advanced division courses in the same building, and three years later 1,550 out of the 2,898 primary schools in Scotland were providing such courses, but only 43 of them were separate schools for advanced division pupils. An attempt was made, however, to give the courses a favourable staffing-ratio, however unfavourable the actual teaching conditions might be. By the regulations of 1923, whereas the maximum number of pupils permitted below the qualifying stage was sixty (mercifully reduced to fifty, five years later), the advanced division courses were given parity with the first three years of secondary schools with a permitted maximum of forty pupils per teacher and half that number for practical and laboratory subjects. It should be noted, however, that in the later years of full secondary schools the number was reduced to thirty even for general subjects. To facilitate attendance at the courses many education authorities took advantage of the provisions of the education acts to establish residential accommodation for pupils from outlying areas, and by 1936 there were seventeen hostels for the purpose in Scotland.

The general aims of advanced division courses remained substantially the same as those of the supplementary courses they displaced, but a definite attempt was made to introduce a curriculum both longer and broader in content than before. It was designed to continue and develop the pupil's general education, not only in the intellectual but also in the moral and physical spheres, and at the same time to include a practical element with a broad vocational bias. Thus every course had to provide for training in morals and citizenship, music, physical exercises and certain subjects of a general education, in particular English, history, geography, science and mathematics. Science covered physics, chemistry and biology or rural science; mathematics comprised arithmetic, geometry and algebra, except in the case of courses for girls of less than 3 years' duration, when only the first was provided. After due provision had been made for these basic subjects, the remaining time was to be devoted to practical training in a variety of courses with a bias towards some occupation or vocation. These might include drawing, one or more of a number of 'practical' subjects either technical (such as technical drawing, benchwork, mechanics, navigation, gardening and agriculture) or domestic (such as needlework, design, dressmaking, cookery, laundrywork and housewifery), and (in courses of not less than 2 years) commercial subjects and a foreign language.

The content of this part of the curriculum was necessarily largely determined by the individual pupil's vocational ambitions and by the probable length of his school life, but the academic bias of Scottish education naturally caused the three year literary course including a language other than English to be preferred, at least to begin with. Even as late as 1934 the Department reported that this course still predominated, although there had been a gradual development of more technical, commercial, domestic and rural courses as well. The regulations for the two Day School Certificates to which the courses led were promulgated in departmental circulars of December 1923 (for the Higher) and January 1924 (for the Lower). Both were to be awarded on the recommendation of H.M.

Inspectors and with the Department's authority, to pupils leaving school, but from the first the Lower Certificate was actually issued by the education authority or managing body and not by the Department itself.

The method of examination for both certificates was more or less the same and was based on school records, test results and teachers' estimates according to the new techniques of the day. For the Day School Certificate (Lower) no hard and fast requirements were laid down, except that it might be awarded only after the successful completion of an advanced division course of not less than two years' duration, whereas the Merit Certificate which it replaced had been awarded after one year in a supplementary course. After 1933 even the recommendation of H.M. Inspectors was dispensed with and complete responsibility for the award of the certificate was delegated to the local education authorities.

The Day School Certificate (Higher), on the other hand, was a distinctly stiffer proposition. Under the original regulations all candidates had to be presented in not less than five subjects, including either a foreign language or mathematics, and in addition they were required to take a short written paper set by the Department to gauge general intelligence and assess power of comprehending and using English. This certificate replaced the former Intermediate Certificate and was awarded by the Department to pupils who had followed an approved course for three or four years but who were forced to leave school before taking the Leaving Certificate. It was intended to differ from the Intermediate Certificate in being based on a wider curriculum and including a greater variety of practical subjects. For this reason only one written paper was set, in contradistinction to the former certificate, for which all the papers had been written except in the case of such practical subjects as had been permitted. Even so, however, experience indicated that the examinations tended to perpetuate the academic bias, and to encourage increased instruction in non-examinable subjects revised regulations were issued in June 1932 reducing the minimum group to four subjects including English (with history and geography), arithmetic and science or art and crafts.

One problem which the demand for secondary education for all served to accentuate was the case of the non-qualifier who tripped at the hurdle of the selection examination. It had been the custom to retain such pupils in the primary school for successive attempts at an examination they were never likely to succeed in passing, but gradually the Department urged on education authorities the adoption of a policy of 'age-pass' at 13. Particularly after the appearance of the Hadow Report on the education of the adolescent in England in 1926 the so-called 'clean cut' came to be accepted at 12 or 12½ whether the pupil passed in the qualifying examination or not. This, of course, necessitated a special or modified curriculum to meet the needs of non-qualifiers at the post-primary stage, but resolute efforts were made to overcome this difficulty in most areas. Notwithstanding all this progress, however, disinterested observers have been unfavourably impressed by the retention of the time-honoured 'tawse' or strap as an instrument of corporal punishment in Scottish schools, and in general discipline has been stricter and more formal than in England.

The greatly extended powers, particularly in the matter of granting bursaries, conferred upon education authorities by the act of 1918 were found by experience to necessitate a revision of educational endowments in the country, and so a departmental committee under the chairmanship of Lord Mackenzie was appointed by the Secretary of State on 7th April 1927 to consider the existing position regarding the administration and application of educational endowments in Scotland. Having regard to legislative changes and developments affecting the educational system since 1882, when endowments had last been reviewed by statute, the committee was invited to suggest what kind of powers should be given to any executive commission set up by Parliament to deal with educational endowments and to lay down principles guiding the exercise of such powers.

With exemplary despatch the committee produced their report by August of the same year. They accepted the view that the purpose of an educational endowment was to confer on the recipients an educational advantage which they would not otherwise obtain. At the same time, they recognized that there were very few educational purposes to which rate-aid might not now be applied, but in consequence they considered it all the more incumbent upon those responsible for the administration of educational endowments to seek fresh outlets for their funds. As an indication of the enlarged scope of the educational services, they suggested for the consideration of trustees the provision of halls of residence for students, central institutions, hostels for school children, adult education, playing fields, youth clubs, and training schools for nurses. They recommended the appointment of an executive commission, consisting as in 1882 of seven members, for a period of at least five years; they suggested the further possibility of the Department thereafter assuming some kind of permanent supervision, rather as the Board of Education had taken over certain functions from the Charity Commissioners in England, except that in the case of university endowments the Universities Committee of the Privy Council should act in this way.

All educational endowments should be compulsorily brought under the jurisdiction of the commissioners, with the exception of those founded after 1920, or administered by university bodies, or applicable to theological purposes, or in the hands of the Carnegie Trustees for the Universities of Scotland, which should be exempt, unless the respective governing bodies should intimate their consent in writing. Otherwise, the commissioners should be given full powers to reorganize educational endowments, group and combine them, modify and alter the purposes to which they were applicable, and prepare draft schemes for applying the revenue to such educational purposes, mental or physical, moral or social, as should best suit the public interest and the existing state of society. Nevertheless, the committee likewise urged that the commissioners should have due regard to the spirit of the founder's intention, either as expressed in the original trust-deed or as later modified in an approved scheme, and further that they should not overlook the interests of the localities to which the endowments naturally belonged.

Effect was given to most of these proposals in an act passed in the following year and overtly modelled on the Educational Endowments Act of 1882. By the Educational Endowments (Scotland) Act of 1928 His Majesty was empowered to appoint a commission to carry out the purposes of the act, save that the number of commissioners was to be increased to nine and the duration of their powers reduced to three years, unless extended by Parliament. This limitation proved in practice to be exceedingly inconvenient, and no fewer than two additional acts were required to prolong the commission's existence. In most other respects, however, the Mackenzie Committee's proposals were more or less literally incorporated in the statute and the commissioners were granted wide discretion in altering purposes, applying capital or income, grouping, amalgamating or combining endowments, altering constitutions of governing bodies and uniting existing governing bodies. They were directed to have regard to the spirit of the founder's intentions as recommended, to bear in mind the interests of localities, to consider the possibility of effecting economies in administration by judicious grouping, and to pay due attention to the interests of particular categories of persons, whether as inhabitants of a particular area or as belonging to a particular social class, when modifying the privileges or advantages of such people in any of their schemes.

Their powers were not to extend to any of the four excepted types of endowment specified in the original committee's recommendations, unless with the consent of the governing body concerned. Inspection and audit were to be obligatory for any school sharing in an endowment or scheme dealt with by the commissioners, and all endowments of less than £50 annual value, attached to grant-aided or public schools, might be approved by the Department without need of an order in council or parliamentary sanction. The Commissioners were instructed to submit an annual report to the Department and their powers were to cease on 31st December 1931. Thereafter, the Department should have like powers regarding the framing of schemes for the future government and management of endowments, except in the case of university endowments or the Carnegie Trust, where the appropriate authority would be the Universities Committee of the Privy Council. Finally, the act was to come into force on 1st January 1929. A royal warrant appointing nine commissioners under the chairmanship of the Earl of Elgin was duly issued on 11th December 1928.

These commissioners found themselves faced with a task no less exacting than that tackled by the Balfour of Burleigh Commission of 1882. The duration of their powers was extended for three years by a second act of 1931 and for a further two years by a retrospective act of 1935. Thus their labours continued until 31st December 1936, but scarcely a single member, apart from the indefatigable chairman, lasted the course. The work done, however, was invaluable and the commissioners published eight annual reports. The act of 1935, in addition, introduced certain minor modifications as regards endowments. The commissioners' attention, for instance, was to be directed to the need for continuing the provision from endowments of competitive bursaries at universities, central institutions and training colleges. Then, except for draft schemes already approved under the original act of 1928, a period of 20 years was to elapse from the date of the trust deed in the case of endowments to be dealt with in future. Lastly, the Department was empowered to disapprove schemes submitted by the commissioners, after which all powers of the latter were to cease to extend to the particular endowment concerned.

Among the excepted categories of endowment only the University of Edinburgh availed itself of the permissive powers under the original act and submitted draft schemes dealing with 85 endowments for the consideration of the commissioners. Altogether, the commissioners reviewed a total of 1,540 endowments, 1,296 of which they included in 129 schemes representing an annual revenue of £354,808. Among the objects which they considered worthy of support from endowment funds, in addition to those already proposed, were the following: school meals for children in country districts, school libraries, facilities for practical experience of trades and occupations, post-graduate scholarships tenable at English and foreign universities, travel grants, school excursions, the institution of special lectures, the provision of nursery schools, a limited expenditure on bursaries, and the supply of food, boots and clothing in the case of necessitous children. The commissioners roughly classified the endowments dealt with into seven categories and estimated that, including money from public funds and other sources, they disposed of as much as £746,749 per annum. This sum was distributed approximately in the following way: education areas, £112,000; special bursaries, £32,500; central institutions, £142,000; schools, £362,000; homes and orphanages,

£49,000; miscellaneous, £28,500; university endowments, £21,000.

Perhaps the most significant development which emerged from the results of their investigations was the extent to which endowed schools had been increasingly unable to meet the rising costs of education. Out of 158 endowed schools dealt with under the Endowment Acts of 1878 and 1882, 77 had been closed down, 47 put under the management of school boards and 34 placed under *ad hoc* governing bodies. Selkirk High School had subsequently been added to the last group, but in the meantime the number gradually dwindled to 13. Of the other 22 schools, 5 had either been closed down or transferred to the local authority under powers contained in the relative scheme, 3 had been transferred by the Court of Session, 9 by the act of 1908, 4 by the act of 1918 and 1 (Allan Glen's School) by a Provisional Order confirmed by Parliament. Even of the 13 hardy survivors, apart from Fettes College which was in a class by itself, only George Heriot's School and the four schools of the Edinburgh Merchant Company, though receiving assistance from the Education (Scotland) Fund, were not aided by their local authority. The only alteration made by the commissioners in this respect was the transference of Dollar Academy from the Clackmannan education authority to an independent governing body. As the basis of their reorganization of endowments the commissioners adopted the education area scheme, in twenty-one cases entrusting the administration to the local authority itself and in the other fourteen establishing an *ad hoc* governing body to administer it. Their final report appeared on 10th March 1937.

Meanwhile two other noteworthy developments had taken place. The first of these was the foundation of the Scottish Council for Research in Education, which, though not a statutory body, has undoubtedly exerted a profound influence on Scottish education. Interest in educational research had been stimulated by the institution of degrees in education at the close of the First World War, and in 1919 the Educational Institute of Scotland established a special Research Committee. In May 1927 the Association of Directors of Education in Scotland approached this committee with a view to collaboration in educational research and the idea of a research council was born. A further approach was made to the Department and the first meeting of the Council was held on 23rd June 1928. In December 1932 the Research Council was formally incorporated, comprising, in addition to a Director, 3 representatives of the Association of County Councils in Scotland, 2 representatives of the Association of Counties of Cities, 8 representatives of the Educational Institute, 5 representatives of the Association of Directors of Education, 2 representatives of the National Committee for the Training of Teachers, 4 representatives of the training centres, 4 representatives of the universities, 2 representatives of the Scottish branch of the British Psychological Society, and 2 representatives of the Association of School Medical Officers. It had thus a widely representative character, and it was supremely fortunate in obtaining the services of a distinguished educationist, Dr. R. R. Rusk, as its first Director. By 1946 the Research Council had been responsible for some twenty-five publications, generally of a very high standard of scholarship and maintaining a nice balance between the historical and experimental aspects of educational research.

The other development of the period was a revision of the law relating to delinquent children by the Children and Young Persons (Scotland) Act of 1932. This measure amended the Children Act of 1908 and abolished the distinction between the former reformatory and industrial schools. Both types of school were renamed 'approved schools' and it was left to the Department to classify them according to the age or religious persuasion of the pupils, or the character of the instruction given in them. The Department was directed to approve existing certified reformatory and industrial schools and might also approve for the purposes of the act any day industrial school. Children under ten were not in general to be sent to an approved school unless a fit person of their own religious persuasion could not be found to undertake their care, and for the purposes of the act a 'young person' was defined as one between 14 and 17 years of age. Children might in the first instance be detained at an approved school for a period of three years or until the age of 15, and young persons for the same period or until the age of 19. By section 38 of the act education authorities were empowered to provide approved schools if they could satisfy the Department that the proposed expenditure was reasonable and that a deficiency of approved school accommodation existed in their area. In general, however, except in Glasgow, little advantage was taken of this, and the majority of approved schools in Scotland have remained under the control of voluntary managers, being directly financed by the Department. The act also regulated the employment of children, and empowered education authorities to make additional by-laws restricting the employment not only of children of statutory school age but, under certain safeguards, even of young persons up to 18. The statutory provisions relating to children and young persons which were still in force were consolidated in another Children and Young Persons Act of 1937 but the educational requirements were unaffected.

The financial crisis of 1931 caused a temporary set-back to educational expansion but the underlying ideal of secondary education for all was not lost sight of. The reorganization of post-primary education in England, having been undertaken at a later date by the Board of Education's acceptance of the Hadow Report in 1928, was much more seriously affected; but by the beginning of

1934 a measure of recovery had been achieved and by 1936 an education act had been passed not only sanctioning certain financial agreements with voluntary schools in England 'for the benefit of senior children', but even proposing to put into effect the clause of the 1918 act raising the school leaving age to 15, as from 1st September 1939. At the same time the opportunity was taken of securing legislation for modifying the educational position in Scotland. By the Education (Scotland) Act of 1936 provision was likewise made for bringing into operation section 14 of the act of 1918, in virtue of which the school leaving age would be raised to 15 as from 1st September 1939. The age of exemption was to be raised from twelve to fourteen, but local authorities were empowered to grant certificates of exemption to children over fourteen for what was euphemistically termed 'beneficial employment', though they were directed to have due regard to such considerations as the hours of work, opportunities for further education and time available for recreation, before doing so.

Perhaps the most important achievement was contained in section 11, which gave implicit recognition to the demand for universal secondary education. The terminology of section 34 of the act of 1908 defining an 'intermediate' and a 'secondary' school was to be replaced by the single label 'secondary education', covering all instruction approved by the Department in such subjects as should be recognized by them as suitable for pupils who had reached the stage marking the conclusion of the primary course. This decision represents the culmination of the reorganization of 1923, and it is in line with the Scottish educational tradition which tended to favour an 'end-on' articulation of schools rather than an overlapping of 'primary' schools taking pupils up to 15 with 'secondary' schools receiving other children from the age of twelve. Finally, with regard to teachers, a manifest source of potential injustice was removed by extending to certificated teachers in the service of grant-aided endowed schools and demonstration schools managed by provincial committees, which by an oversight had previously escaped the net, the same privileges regarding dismissal as were enjoyed by other teachers under sections 21 of the 1908 and 24 of the 1918 education acts.

The logical implications of section 11 of the act were the abolition of a dual code of regulations and the renaming of the former Advanced Divisions. In anticipation of the raising of the leaving age the Department issued a circular at the end of 1937 announcing certain changes in the conditions for award of the Leaving Certificate in and after 1940, and these were incorporated in the code of 1939, which contained the Department's requirements relating to all types of school in a single set of regulations. The principal changes were the separation of history from English as a subject in its own right, and a dispensation from the necessity of presenting all candidates in either mathematics or science and a foreign language. Instead, every candidate was required to take a paper in arithmetic and the minimum group was raised to two higher and three lower subjects, including English on the higher standard and either history or geography on at least the lower, exclusive of this additional paper. The Day School Certificate (lower) was abolished entirely, on the assumption that all would complete at least three years post-primary education, and the Day School Certificate (higher) was replaced by a new Junior Leaving Certificate, awarded by the Department along similar lines to its predecessor but without the general written paper formerly required.[1] At the same time the Leaving Certificate, which had for many years been popularly, though unofficially, qualified

[1] Owing to the outbreak of war the operation of the Junior Leaving Certificate was suspended, but a number of local authorities instituted a Junior Secondary Certificate instead.

by the prefix 'higher', was redesignated the Senior Leaving Certificate to avoid confusion.

A similar nomenclature was applied to all post-primary schools, which came to be known as Senior or Junior Secondary Schools according as they provided a five or three year course of post-primary education. The adoption of this terminology was later criticized by the Advisory Council on Education in Scotland as conveying a suggestion of inferiority in the case of the so-called 'Junior' Secondary School, and some authorities have endeavoured to develop the system of omnibus secondary schools incorporating both types within one organization, though the English 'multilateral' school proper has never been favoured in Scotland. In fact, however, while these modifications were introduced to meet the new situation, the central and essential condition of their success was largely nullified by the outbreak of the Second World War two days after the raising of the school leaving age. Retrospective legislation was hurriedly prepared, and by the Education (Emergency) (Scotland) Act of 12th October 1939 the relative section of the act of 1936 was repealed and any education authority which had incurred expenditure in that connection was indemnified.

CHAPTER XIV

THE PRESENT POSITION

THE outbreak of war subjected the educational system of the country to considerable strain, partly on account of the evacuation scheme and partly on account of the conscription of male teachers and the requisitioning of school buildings for military purposes. The evacuation scheme, though on the whole a failure, was not without some benefits: in particular, many town children thrived under rural conditions as never before, and many teachers, through increased calls upon their initiative, learned to adopt a more realistic method of approach to their work. But the lack of proper school buildings and the shortages of staff caused grave dislocation of the educational services.

Both the evacuees and those who remained at home in the vulnerable areas were affected. In the reception areas, even when the children were accompanied by their teachers, the existing educational facilities were often inadequate to meet the increased demands made upon them, and in the vulnerable areas schools were frequently closed down and the buildings taken over by other organizations. Consequently, those children who were not evacuated were left without any educational provision at all, and their number was quickly swelled by the return of a large percentage of the evacuees. To add to the confusion, the age of reservation of male teachers from liability for military service was raised from 25 to 30 in the autumn of 1940 and by the beginning of 1941 had been raised to 35 except for those in key positions. The result was that for a time all attempts to enforce school attendance were abandoned, but as early as February 1940 it had become clear that evacuation must in future be regarded as a strictly limited operation and fresh efforts were being made to restore the *status quo* in the urban areas. The stress of war began to bring with it the realization that the nation's greatest asset lay in the youth of the country, and the attention of those in authority was directed to what came to be called 'educational reconstruction'. The earliest concrete example of this was the institution of the Youth Service.

Already, in September 1939, the Board of Education in England had set up a National Youth Committee to co-ordinate the efforts of voluntary organizations for youth welfare, such as the Y.M.C.A., the Y.W.C.A., the Boy Scout and Girl Guide movements, and youth clubs run by religious bodies. In November 1939 the Board issued a circular urging local education authorities to establish properly constituted youth committees in their areas to provide opportunities for the social and physical development of boys and girls between 14 and 20 who had ceased full-time education. In March 1940 the Board agreed to make grants covering 50% of local expenditure on the Youth Service, and three months later formally recognized the Service as a province of further education. In due course the movement was extended to Scotland, and in September 1942 the Department recommended education authorities to assume responsibility for developing a Youth Service in their areas, to set up a Youth Council to advise the education committee on matters concerning the needs of youth and to establish in addition Local Youth Panels to foster the scheme in their own districts. In March 1943 this was followed by the action of the Secretary of State in setting up a Scottish Youth Advisory Committee, which in May 1945 produced a significant report on 'The Needs of Youth in these Times'. In England also the National Youth Committee had been replaced by a Youth Advisory Council in 1942.

Meanwhile, in 1941, the President of the Board of Education had issued what was called a 'Green Book' to local education authorities, teachers' organizations and other bodies, inviting comments on, among other matters, proposals for raising the school leaving age, for abolishing fees in secondary schools and for the recruitment and training of teachers. In the same year he appointed a committee of the Secondary School Examinations Council under Sir Cyril Norwood to consider suggested changes in the secondary school curriculum and the question of examinations in relation to it. In 1942 a departmental committee under Sir Arnold McNair was appointed to investigate the supply and recruitment of teachers and youth leaders, and another committee under Lord Fleming (a senator of the College of Justice in Scotland) was set up to consider the question of extending the association between the Public Schools and the general educational system. In July 1943 the response to the Green Book appeared in the form of the famous white paper on 'Educational Reconstruction' and on 3rd August 1944 a new education act was passed for England and Wales.

The currents of educational reform were somewhat slower in being set in motion in Scotland, but as a preliminary the Advisory Council on Education in Scotland was reconstituted in November 1942 and there followed a spate of stimulating reports. They dealt with compulsory day continuation classes, training for citizenship, training of teachers, grants for adult education and technical education, and culminated fittingly in the outstanding studies on primary education in 1946 and secondary education in 1947. In February 1943 the Association of Directors of Education, and in June of the same year the Reconstruction

Committee of the Educational Institute, published proposals for reconstruction, under the titles of *Education in Scotland* and *The Scottish School* respectively. In spite of this lead, difficulties and delays were encountered in preparing a Scottish education bill, and on the dissolution of the Coalition Government two years later it had not yet passed through all its stages. Unfortunately, too, Mr. Thomas Johnston, the author of the measure, withdrew with his party, and it seemed possible that the bill might be dropped altogether. This, however, was inconceivable in the case of a country so concerned about her educational standards as Scotland, and the two associations brought pressure to bear on Scottish M.P.s to complete the outstanding formalities. Eventually, on 15th June 1945, the bill became law during the brief reign of the 'Caretaker Government'.

It was primarily designed to apply to Scotland the new principles set forth in the English act of the previous year and was essentially only a patchwork piece of legislation. Nevertheless, it was a sufficiently complex measure, comprising 89 sections and six schedules. The act was set out in five parts, which dealt with the provision of education by education authorities, the rights and duties of parents and the functions of education authorities in relation to individual pupils, administration and staffing, independent schools, and a number of general provisions. To simplify the administrative position it was deemed desirable in the following year to consolidate all the existing legislation relating to education in Scotland, including the Education (Scotland) Act of 1945 and the unrepealed portions of all previous enactments on the subject. The Education (Scotland) Act of 1946, which governs the present position, thus introduced no new principle but merely brought together existing ones in a form convenient for administrative purposes.

It is essential, however, to consider in some detail the

main provisions of the act of 1945. As in England, the statutory system was organized in three progressive stages, to be known as primary, secondary and further education, and it was made the duty of education authorities to secure throughout their areas adequate and efficient provision of all forms of each, including the teaching of Gaelic in Gaelic-speaking areas. Primary education was described as progressive elementary education in such subjects as might be prescribed in the code, having regard to the age, ability and aptitude of the pupils concerned, and it was specifically declared to include nursery school education from the age of two. Secondary education was to comprise progressive courses of instruction of such length and in such subjects as might be considered appropriate both to the age, ability and aptitude of pupils promoted from primary schools and to the period of time they might be expected to remain at school. Further education was to have two branches. The first would be compulsory part-time courses to be given in 'junior colleges' (corresponding to 'county colleges' in England) to young persons, with a view to developing their various aptitudes and capacities and preparing them for the responsibilities of citizenship. The second would be voluntary courses of instruction, and leisure-time occupation in organized cultural training and recreative activities for persons over school age.[1]

So far as the provision of nursery school and secondary education was concerned, the criterion of 'adequacy' was to be, in the one case, a sufficient number of children (whose parents should desire such education for them) to form a school or class of reasonable size, and, in the other, a sufficient variety of courses to allow a parent to select one from which his child might show reasonable promise of profiting. At the same time the parent's right to select a course of secondary education from which his child, in the opinion of the education authority, showed no reason-

[1] The term 'adult education' is not specifically mentioned in the Act.

able promise of profiting was rejected, with the safeguard of appeal to the Secretary of State. As in the act of 1918, education authorities were required to submit schemes for approval by the Secretary of State. In drawing them up they were directed to have regard to the expediency of providing boarding education where that might be desirable and, in the case of further education, to the need for providing adequate technical education and establishing residential colleges for other forms of continuative education.

The Youth Service was given statutory recognition by imposing on education authorities the duty of including in their educational provision adequate facilities for recreation and social and physical training for persons for whom any of the statutory forms of education were being provided. They were further empowered to provide suitable clothing for physical exercise for any pupils in attendance at schools or junior colleges under their management. In section 4, section 68 of the act of 1872, which had limited the times during which religious observance in schools might be practised and religious instruction given, was repealed, leaving the schools complete freedom in that respect. By section 6 an education authority was empowered to provide a child guidance service, the function of which should be to study handicapped, backward and difficult children, and to give to teachers and parents advice about appropriate methods of education and training in such cases. This was an important concession since most of the previously existing child guidance clinics had been provided by the universities and training centres under the auspices of the Scottish Child Guidance Council, though the importance of the work had long suggested the need for a permanent organization. Under section 10 authority was given for any local authority, which was at the same time an authority under the Mental Deficiency Acts and the Education Acts, to combine institutions for mental defectives with special schools, but the expediency of maintaining schools for the mentally and physically handicapped in the same building is perhaps open to question.

In general the education provided in public schools and junior colleges was to be without payment of fees, but the customary proviso allowing the retention of a limited number of fee-paying primary and secondary schools by local authorities was continued under the control of the Department. This was in direct contrast to the policy in England, where only direct-grant schools were permitted to continue charging fees, and it seems to imply that Scottish democracy is less suspect where educational provision is concerned. Free education was to include books, stationery, mathematical instruments and the like, and local authorities were permitted to make similar provisions for pupils in their area attending educational establishments other than public schools. They might also give financial assistance to any university for the purpose of improving the facilities for further education available in their area.

In Part II of the act education authorities were instructed to accept as a guiding principle that, while unreasonable public expense should be avoided, pupils were to be educated in accordance with the wishes of their parents. They were required to prepare and submit for the approval of the Secretary of State a 'promotion scheme' showing the method to be adopted for promoting pupils from primary to secondary schools and also for reaching a decision about the kind of course a pupil was likely to benefit from. At the same time a parent's duty towards his child was redefined as being 'to provide efficient education for him suitable to his age, ability and aptitude', and all exemption for beneficial employment was abolished. At last the school leaving age was to be definitely raised to 15, on 1st April 1946 or within one year thereafter, but even then this decision was not put into effect until 1st April 1947. The Secretary of State was authorized to raise it still further to sixteen as soon as might be practicable, but in our present economic circumstances the likelihood of this is remote.

The same applies to the full-scale provision of junior colleges, designed to supply a better integrated form of compulsory part-time education between the school leaving age (whether fifteen or sixteen) and eighteen than the former continuation classes. Approximately the same aggregate total of 330 hours of instruction was laid down, but the method of receiving it was more strictly regulated. One whole day or two half days per week during 44 weeks, or, if more convenient, one continuous period of 8 weeks or two of 4 weeks, were the only approved forms such attendance might take. Again the onus of attending was to be placed on the young person himself and not on his parents. So that all would be in a position to avail themselves to the full of these educational facilities, local authorities were empowered to defray any necessary fees and expenses in the case of school children and to grant scholarships and other allowances to those over school age. In this case, however, the power was to be exercised under regulations made by the Secretary of State, which might require the authority to leave out of account in the assessment of applicants any scholarship gained in open competition or any award made by the Carnegie Trustees for the Universities of Scotland. There was some need for a provision of this kind, in view of considerable inequalities and lack of uniformity between local authorities in granting university bursaries under previous legislation.

Physical well-being was not forgotten: all authorities were obliged to supply milk and a midday meal for those in attendance at schools and junior colleges whenever in session, and they were given powers of providing additional meals at other times of day and even of making similar provision for pupils at schools not under their own management. Account was also taken of medical inspection, supervision and treatment: all authorities must provide for periodic medical inspection of pupils in attendance at public schools and junior colleges as well as make available for them comprehensive free medical treatment (unless parents objected to their children receiving it), and they might extend such facilities to pupils in other educational establishments. Lastly, in the case of any child enrolled at a school, an education authority was empowered to restrict employment where it might be prejudicial to the child's health or to his obtaining full benefit from the educational facilities provided.

In Part III of the act one of the most important provisions was the section compelling every authority to appoint a Director of Education. After the act of 1918, it is true, the very first circular issued by the re-christened Scottish Education Department had urged on the new authorities the importance of appointing a full-time executive officer, and the great majority had done so. But in some instances, such as Renfrewshire, the chairman himself had for long carried on the main administrative duties without the assistance of a Director. In view of the increasing complexity of administration such arrangements were to be deprecated in the interests of complete efficiency, and as a consequence all authorities were instructed to set out in the schemes for the exercise of their educational functions what specific powers and duties they proposed to delegate to their chief education officer.

As regards the training and remuneration of teachers, section 49 granted statutory recognition to the National Committee and the Committees of Management, set up by Departmental minute after the act of 1918, as well as to the reconstituted Provincial Committees. By section 50 the former minimum national salary scales were abolished in favour of standard scales to be prescribed in regulations drawn up by the Secretary of State. Before making such regulations, however, he was instructed to have regard to any recommendations put forward by the National Joint Council. The new standard scales might be made retrospective to 1st April 1945 and all local authorities were compelled to pay salaries in accordance with them except in the case of unqualified teachers. They were forbidden to exceed them, however, to prevent the wealthier authorities and endowed schools from outbidding the others. No woman was to be disqualified from teaching in any public school or junior college, or to be dismissed from her employment, by reason only of marriage. In teachers' superannuation certain minor adjustments were also authorized.

A duty was laid upon the Secretary of State to carry out periodic inspection of all schools and junior colleges, but religious instruction was expressly exempted from this requirement. The cost of inspection was to be remitted for endowed schools, but not (where applied for) in the case of private schools. The Secretary of State was empowered to make payments out of the Education (Scotland) Fund, *inter alia*, for the purpose of promoting educational research, and this power has been acknowledged by the Department as implying the granting of financial assistance to the Research Council.

Part IV dealt with the question of registering independent schools as a means of ensuring certain minimum standards of staffing and accommodation. Such a problem is probably less acute in Scotland than in England, but it was proposed to regulate the keeping of these schools by requiring registration after an appointed day, with the right of appeal to statutory Independent Schools Tribunals in the event of a grievance. In Part V provision was likewise to be made for the registration of all existing educational endowments, other than those vested in universities, theological institutions or the Carnegie Trustees, and of all fresh endowments within one year of the date of coming into operation. This was a step which had been strongly urged by the Elgin Commission of 1928-36. Education authorities were empowered to make provision for conducting or assisting research in their area and to organize conferences for the discussion of questions relating to education. Finally, in section 89, power was given to the Secretary of State to determine the appointed days on which the various provisions of the act were to be brought into operation, except that dealing with raising the school leaving age to 15 and those governing attendance at junior colleges, which were to come into force not later than 3 years thereafter. As has been indicated, however, this last objective has not yet been achieved.

Such, then, in brief outline are the main contents of the Education (Scotland) Act of 1945, of which, as of its English equivalent, it may well be said that it makes possible as important and substantial an advance in public education as the country has ever known. The present position, as already explained, is governed by the consolidating act of 1946, which, by a curious coincidence, was passed almost exactly two hundred and fifty years after its first counterpart, and constitutes an impressive comparison with its modest predecessor of 1696. In it the five parts of the act of 1945 are increased to seven by bringing together under separate heads the existing regulations relating to teachers' superannuation and the reorganization of endowments, while the number of sections is extended to 144 and that of the schedules to eight, which is indicative indeed of the complexity of modern educational administration.

Nominally the supreme authority is still the shadowy Committee of Council on Education in Scotland, consisting of some six or seven members of the Privy Council, of whom four—the Lord President, the Secretary of State for Scotland, the First Lord of the Treasury and the Lord

Advocate—hold office *ex officiis*, while the remainder are appointed from time to time by order in council as vacancies occur. The effective power, however, is vested by statute in the Secretary of State, who, as Vice-President, is the responsible minister, and the day to day work is performed by the Scottish Education Department, which is an integral part of the organization of the Scottish Office. The headquarters of the Department are in Edinburgh, at St. Andrews House, and there the Permanent Secretary carries on his duties, but a liaison branch with a Deputy Secretary in charge is still maintained at the Scottish Office in London. To assist the Secretary of the Department with the vast quantity of work now devolving upon the officials of the central authority, there are in addition an Under Secretary and seven Assistant Secretaries.

Midway between the Department and the practical work of the schools is the inspectorate, and for the purpose of inspection the country is parcelled out in four 'divisions', the Northern, Southern, Western and Highland, with their respective headquarters at Aberdeen, Edinburgh, Kilmacolm and Strathpeffer.[1] At the head of the hierarchy stands the Senior Chief Inspector, who usually makes the training colleges his main concern. In charge of each of the four divisions there is a Chief Inspector, and on an equal footing a Staff Inspector of Technical Education. Next come the nineteen 'districts' into which the divisions are subdivided, each with one or more Inspectors. There are, besides, specialist inspectors of mining education, approved schools, physical training, music, domestic subjects (in this case all women) and the school meals service, and a number of liaison officers for social and recreational services. In comparison with the position in England, the work of the inspectorate is in-

[1] From 15th August 1952 this number was increased to five: South-Eastern, South-Western, Western, North-Eastern and Highland.

creased by a major share in the task of conducting the Leaving Certificate examinations, delegated in England to eight university examining bodies, and by the fact that no part of its business of inspecting the schools is undertaken by the local authorities, which in England generally employ one or more local inspectors.

Until recently, at least, Scotland has been distinguished by a greater degree of centralization in the administration of her educational system, though this is probably due rather to size than to a difference in tradition from her southern neighbour. Nevertheless, duties and powers which in the past have frequently been delegated in England to the local authorities, such as those connected with raising the school-leaving age, have more usually in Scotland been vested in the central authority. It is not, however, that the duties and powers of the Department have ever been very clearly defined, but they may be broadly summarized under the heads of inspection, educational provision, finance, teacher training, court of appeal, school accommodation, approved schools, educational endowments, examining and registration. Thus the Department must inspect all schools, including endowed and, where requested, private schools; regulate the provision of all statutory forms of education by local authorities or grant-aided governing bodies; administer the Education (Scotland) Fund and the superannuation of teachers; regulate the training of teachers and determine appropriate salary scales; enquire into cases of dismissal; exercise supervision over the general provision of school accommodation; superintend and maintain approved schools; supervise the working of educational endowments and frame schemes of reorganization; issue Leaving Certificates; and, from an appointed day, register educational endowments and independent schools. In addition, it is the duty of the Department to approve certain schemes proposed by local authorities, relating to matters such as the constitution of their education and school management committees, the co-operation of two or more authorities for specific purposes, the provision to be made in each area for all forms of education, the method of promotion from primary to secondary schools, the granting of bursaries for higher education, and the arrangements for continuation and adult education classes.

On the other hand, as Morgan says, the administration of the educational system of the country implies a partnership between the central and local authorities. The powers and duties of the latter may be summarized under the heads of school accommodation, employment of teachers, school attendance, additional services, special provision, health services, equality of opportunity, administration of bequests, contributions and miscellaneous. Thus, local authorities must provide school buildings, acquire land and maintain schools; appoint and dismiss teachers, and remunerate them at prescribed rates of salary; compel school attendance, settle dates of commencing and leaving school, and grant exemptions; supply nursery schools, child guidance and (by agreement with the Ministry of Labour) vocational guidance services, and social and recreational facilities; provide for the education of defective, blind or deaf, and special children; make provision for medical inspection and treatment, and supply milk, school meals and clothing; arrange for conveying children to school, establish hostels and make grants for maintenance or fees; receive gifts for schools and take over endowed institutions; contribute towards the upkeep of independent schools, central institutions, training colleges and universities; provide books and stationery in schools, maintain libraries in counties, grant pensions to administrative officials and raise capital loans. Even so, the exercise of some of these functions requires the sanction of the Department, such as the discontinuance of any school, the establishment of a hostel, the provision of a special school, the determination of dates relating to school attendance, the transfer of an endowed or denominational school, the making of contributions to outside institutions and the raising of capital loans.

At the time of the passing of the 1946 act there were in Scotland some 15 schools equivalent (though not so designated) to the 'direct-grant' schools in England, that is to say, in receipt of grants direct from the Secretary of State and not through an education authority, although many were also subsidized by their local authority. Some of these were for boys, others for girls, and a few were mixed. Seven independent boys' schools and one of the direct-grant schools were represented on the Headmasters' Conference, and two or three of the more exclusive girls' schools were included, with their sister establishments in England, in the Girls' School Year Book. There were still only the four ancient universities, but there was a considerable demand for the founding of a fifth, to relieve the existing pressure, and a strong separatist movement of Dundee from St. Andrews.[1]

The sixth schedule of the act enumerated seventeen central institutions, offering a sound diversification of courses. These were: (*a*) technical colleges at Edinburgh, Glasgow and Aberdeen, a combined technical college and art school at Dundee, and the Scottish Woollen Technical College at Galashiels; (*b*) schools of art at Edinburgh and Glasgow; (*c*) colleges of agriculture at Edinburgh, Glasgow and Aberdeen; (*d*) veterinary colleges at Edinburgh and Glasgow; (*e*) colleges of domestic science at Edinburgh and Glasgow: (*f*) a commercial college at Glasgow; (*g*) Leith Nautical College; and (*h*) the Royal Scottish Academy of Music. Besides these there were the Royal Colleges of Physicians and Surgeons at Edinburgh and the

[1] The relations between Dundee and St. Andrews were the subject of a departmental committee under Lord Cooper in 1949 and of a Royal Commission under Lord Tedder in 1951. A bill to produce a more unified type of university was introduced into the House of Lords on 26th November 1952.

Royal Faculty of Physicians and Surgeons at Glasgow, providing undergraduate teaching in medicine and dentistry. At Dundee the dental hospital had been incorporated in the University of St. Andrews in 1937, and there was a movement by the universities at both Edinburgh and Glasgow to assume responsibility not only for all the undergraduate medical and dental teaching but also for all the veterinary teaching in their respective cities. There were the four training centres for teachers closely associated with the universities, the two denominational Roman Catholic colleges for women at Edinburgh and Glasgow, and the women's physical training college at Dunfermline; but there was talk of establishing a Roman Catholic College for men, and evacuation experience during the war had shown that Aberdeen was a more suitable centre for the physical training college than Dunfermline. Finally, there was the adult education residential college at Newbattle Abbey, opened in 1937 and temporarily requisitioned by the army as a 'Formation College'.

If there are weaknesses in the Scottish educational system—and no doubt its detractors can discern many—they are most notably in the sphere of technical and adult education. Owing to the far wider diffusion of secondary and university education in the past, the need for these specific forms has hitherto perhaps been less pressing than in England, but that does not necessarily condone the lack of adequate provision at the present time. In a sense both may be said to have originated in Scotland, in the lectures given by Birkbeck to the Glasgow mechanics, but since then there has been a clear bifurcation of the movement into its vocational and cultural aspects. Indeed, so far as the vocational aspect is concerned, it is at the secondary level rather than at the adult one that technical education in Scotland is lacking, for her central institutions sustain comparison with English technical colleges. The real lack is an efficient system of intermediate education leading up to them and corresponding to the secondary technical school in England. Technical courses, it is true, are provided in junior secondary and, to some extent, in omnibus senior secondary schools, where technical subjects may even be offered in the Senior Leaving Certificate, but Scotland's strenuous resistance to a highly selective scheme of secondary schools on the lines of the English tripartite system has, on the whole, tended to discourage technical education at the secondary stage.

On the cultural side adult education has gradually come to denote the spare-time voluntary pursuit of learning by those over eighteen years of age with a view to developing their effectiveness as human beings and citizens rather than as technicians. In England this form of education received a great impetus from the university extension movement of the later nineteenth century and the founding of the Workers' Educational Association in 1903. Later the co-operation of the local education authorities was also enlisted, and in 1924 this triple alliance of 'responsible bodies' was specifically recognized by the Board of Education regulations for the provision of adult education classes. In Scotland, on the other hand, the more conservative universities have been slow to develop flourishing extramural departments as in England, and the Workers' Educational Association has obtained at best only a precarious foothold. Nor has the policy of the Department been so congenial to expansion in this direction, for it has limited its support of adult education to the usual 60% of approved expenditure by the local education authorities alone, although they may delegate their functions to voluntary bodies such as the Workers' Educational Association, whereas in England the Ministry of Education has been willing to make special tuition grants of 75% of such expenditure to any of the recognized responsible bodies.

Of recent years there has been an undoubted trend towards assimilating Scottish with English institutions, and the educational system has not remained unaffected. A number of improvements in the school economy, such as the prefect system and a healthy inter-house rivalry, have been imported into many Scottish schools. In other respects they have preserved distinctively Scottish features, such as the use of the strap (instead of the cane) as the normal method of corporal punishment. Even in these days of increasing specialization the old custom of nominating the best all-round pupil as 'dux' of the school is still continued. But in the wider field there are indications that Scotland has lost some of her former initiative. It is true, certainly, that since 1870 Scottish legislation has never preceded but always followed, or at best coincided with, English legislation, but it has been customary for Scottish acts to mark an advance on their English counterparts. Thus the general acts of 1872, 1908, 1918 and 1945 may be said to correspond roughly with those of 1870, 1902, 1918 and 1944, but, while seemingly parallel, the Scottish acts introduced important points of principle only subsequently adopted in England. Similarly, the special measures relating to school attendance passed in 1883, 1901 and 1936 generally implied a higher leaving age or more effective attendance at school than the English acts of 1876-80, 1900 and 1936.

As specific examples we may mention that in primary education the principle of compulsion was accepted in Scotland in 1872 and in England not fully till 1880, the principle of free education in Scotland in 1889 and in England in 1891, and the school leaving age of fourteen in Scotland in 1901 and in England not universally until 1918. In secondary education the right to free schooling was recognized in Scotland in 1918 and in England in 1944, and the reorganization of all post-primary education as secondary was accepted in Scotland in 1936 and in England only in 1944. Some advances, such as the compulsory training of all teachers, which was effected in Scotland as long ago as 1906, and the solution of the problem of 'dual control', which was successfully tackled in Scotland in 1918, have not yet been really squarely faced in England.

On the other hand, it must be admitted that the act of 1945 contains, for the first time, no substantial advance on the English act of 1944. It would appear that Scotland, which had a national system of education when England was merely groping in the dark, has been marking time or even falling behind. This tendency shows itself most notably in a certain lack of experimentation, which forces progressive Scottish educationists such as A. S. Neill to take refuge in the more responsive atmosphere of England. The traditional 'sound learning' which characterizes Scottish education is not to be despised, but there is a danger of its becoming a closed system. With two hundred and fifty years of steady progress in education behind her, Scotland has good reason to cultivate her distinctive tradition, and her contribution to the educational tradition of Great Britain has not gone unrecognized. In *Freedom in the Educative Society* (1948) Sir Fred Clarke, while claiming that the English tradition has had the main shaping influence in our society, qualifies his statement by conceding: 'It has been a very fortunate thing for us that Scotland, and now increasingly Wales, have had such freedom to cultivate a distinctive tradition, British indeed, but each having traits all its own.'

SELECT BIBLIOGRAPHY

**denotes a work of particular importance*

(i) COMPILATIONS

1. GENERAL:

*Graham Balfour: *The Educational Systems of Great Britain and Ireland* (2nd edition 1903)

S. J. Curtis: *A History of Education in Great Britain* (1948)

W. J. Gibson: *Education in Scotland* (1912)

*J. Kerr: *Scottish Education, School and University* (1910)

*Alexander Morgan: *Rise and Progress of Scottish Education* (1927)

George Stewart: *The Story of Scottish Education* (1927)

2. SPECIAL PERIODS:

*John Edgar: *History of Early Scottish Education* (1893)

G. P. Insh: *School Life in Old Scotland* (1925)

*H. G. Graham: *The Social Life of Scotland in the Eighteenth Century* (1899); particularly Chapters XI to XIII

J. Clarke: *Short Studies in Education in Scotland* (1904)

J. Smith: *Broken Links in Scottish Education* (1913)

3. SPECIAL TYPES:

C. S. Bremner: *Education of Girls and Women in Great Britain* (1897)

*James Grant: *History of the Burgh Schools of Scotland* (1876)

Scottish Council for Research in Education: *Scottish Primary School Organisation* (1939)

*John Strong: *A History of Secondary Education in Scotland* (1909)

*N. A. Wade: *Post-Primary Education in the Primary Schools of Scotland 1872 to 1936* (1939)

*A. Wright: *History of Education and of the Old Parish Schools of Scotland* (1898)

4. PERSONALITIES:

*Alexander Morgan: *Makers of Scottish Education* (1929)

5. Special Aspects:

Irene F. M. Dean: *Scottish Spinning Schools* (1930)

J. Mason: *A History of Scottish Experiments in Rural Education* (1935)

D. K. Wilson: *The History of Mathematical Teaching in Scotland* (1935)

6. Special Regions:

J. C. Jessop: *Education in Angus up to the act of* 1872 (1931)

I. J. Simpson: *Education in Aberdeenshire before* 1872 (1947)

7. Training of Teachers:

L. G. E. Jones: *The Training of Teachers in England and Wales* (1924); makes frequent comparisons with Scotland

*R. R. Rusk: *The Training of Teachers in Scotland—an historical Review* (1928)

8. The Universities:

*Alexander Morgan: *Scottish University Studies* (1933)

A. E. Clapperton: *Ordinances of the Commissioners under the Universities (Scotland) Act,* 1858, *together with Alterations authorized by Orders in Council* (1916)

A. E. Clapperton: *Ordinances of the Commissioners under the Universities (Scotland) Act,* 1889 *and University Court Ordinances to* 31*st December* 1914 (1915)

A. E. Clapperton: *University Court Ordinances* 1915 *to* 1924 (1925)

W. A. Fleming: *University Court Ordinances* 1925 *to* 1947 (1948)

R. G. Cant: *A Short History of the University of St. Andrews* (1946)

J. Coutts: *A History of the University of Glasgow* (1909)

*Sir Alexander Grant: *The Story of the University of Edinburgh* (1884), continued to 1933 under the editorship of A. Logan Turner

R. S. Rait: *The Universities of Aberdeen* (1895)

9. Miscellaneous:

*A. J. Belford: *Centenary Handbook of the Educational Institute of Scotland* (1946)

Scottish Council for Research in Education: *Aims and Activities* (1945)

(ii) Official Reports

1. General:

**Reports of the Royal Commission* (chm. Duke of Argyll) *on Schools in Scotland* (1865-8)

**Reports of a Departmental Committee* (chm. C. S. Parker) *on Certain Questions relating to Education in Scotland* (1888)

2. Post-Primary Education:

*Report of the Commissioners in terms of the 11th Section of the Endowed Institutions (Scotland) Act of 1878 (1881); see also Endowments†

Report of a Departmental Committee (chm. Earl of Elgin) as to the best means of distributing the Grant in aid of Secondary Education (1892)

3. Endowments:

*Reports of Royal Commission (chm. Sir T. E. Colebrooke) on Endowed Schools and Hospitals (1873-5)

Reports of Endowed Institutions Commission (chm. Lord Moncrieff)† (1880-1)

Reports of Educational Endowments Commission (chm. Lord Balfour of Burleigh) (1883-9)

*Report of a Departmental Committee (chm. Lord Mackenzie) on Educational Endowments in Scotland (1927)

Reports of Educational Endowments Commission (chm. Earl of Elgin) (1929-36)

4. Universities:

*Report of the Royal Commission (chm. Earl of Rosebery) on the Universities and Colleges of Scotland (1831)

General Report of the Commissioners (chm. Lord Inglis) under the Universities Act of 1858 (1863)

*Report of the Royal Commissioners (chm. Lord Inglis) appointed to inquire into the Universities of Scotland (1878)

*General Report of the Commissioners (chm. Lord Kinnear) under the Universities Act of 1889 (1900)

(iii) Works of Reference

A. P. Laurie (ed.): The Teacher's Encyclopaedia (1911-12)

P. Monroe (ed.): Cyclopedia of Education (1911-13)

F. Watson (ed.): Encyclopaedia and Dictionary of Education (1922)

Yearbook of Education (1932-40)

(iv) Comparative Studies

Horace Mann: Report of an Educational Tour in Europe and Parts of Great Britain and Ireland (ed. W. B. Hodgson, 1846)

Sir James Kay-Shuttleworth: Public Education (1853)

D. R. Fearon: Report on certain Burgh Schools in Scotland (Vol. VI of The Schools Inquiry Commission) (1868)

Sir Henry Craik: The State in its Relation to Education (3rd edition, 1914)

F. W. Roman: The New Education in Europe (2nd edition, 1930)

(v) ADMINISTRATION

Scottish Education Department: *The Administration of Public Education in Scotland* (1938)
Scottish Education Department: *Scottish Educational Services* (1938)
Scottish Office: *A Handbook on Scottish Administration* (1950)

INDEX

Aberdeen Grammar School, 70
Aberdeen University, 52, 86, 89, 91, 92, 148, 151
King's College, 15
Marischal College, 16
Acland, A. H. D., 113
Acts of Parliament
Blind and Deaf-Mute Children (1890), 175
Children (1908), 181-3; (1932), 219-20
Copyright (1710), 49; (1837), 50
Day Industrial Schools (1893), 182
Defective Children (1906), 175
Education
Scotland: (1872), 61-6, 77-80; (1878), 68, 85; (1883), 108-9; (1897), 187; (1901), 117-8; (1908), 137-8, 168, 175-181; (1918), 168, 183-90; (1936), 221-2; (1945), 227, 228-34; (1946), 227, 234
England: (1870), 61-4; (1876), 65, 108-9, 181; (1891), 113-4; (1900), 117; (1902), 136, 175; (1936), 221; (1944), 226
Endowments (1869), 76; (1878), 67-8, 84; (1882), 122-3; (1928), 215-6
Factory and Workshop (1878), 108
Industrial Schools (various), 181
Local Government (1889), 112-3, 125; (1929), 190-1
Local Taxation Account (1890), 113; (1892), 114, 132; (1898), 135
Parochial Schools (1803), 23-4; (1838), 26; (1861), 32-3
Public Schools Teachers (1882), 207
Reformatory Schools (various), 182
Representation of the People (1868), 97; (1918), 170n
Rescissory (1661), 5, 16
Schools, Plantation of (1633), Founding of (1646), Settling of (1696), 3-5
Secretary for Scotland (1885), 109; of State (1926), 192
Security (1707), 6, 50
Settling Quiet and Peace of Church (1693), 42
Teachers' Superannuation (various), 177-8
Technical Schools (1887), 126; (1892), 131
Universities (1853), 51; (1858), 52, 86-92; (1889), 102, 153-8; (1922), 170; (1932), 171
Visitation (1690), 14, 50
Advisory Council on Education, 188-9, 203, 205, 223, 226
Agriculture, 108, 114, 135, 238
Almond, H. H., 39
Anderson, John, 43
Art, 213, 238
Arts, 17, 48, 92-4, 99-100, 162-3
Ayr Grammar School, 13

Bajans, 17
Bathgate Academy, 39, 76
Bell, Andrew, 39, 139, 146-7

Birkbeck, George, 20, 43
Board of Education for Scotland, 58, 62
Brewster, Sir David, 89
Brougham, Henry (Lord), 25, 29
Bursaries, 123-4, 179, 180-1, 184, 213, 217, 231

Cambridge University, 51, 96, 97, 98, 148
Campbeltown Grammar School, 42
Carnegie Trust: Dunfermline, 197
 Universities, 168, 214, 216, 231, 233
Carstares, William, 18
Central Institutions, 152, 185, 199, 204, 217, 238
Chalmers, Thomas, 28
Child Guidance, 229
Children, Employment of, 108-9, 112, 187, 220, 221, 232
Chrystal, George, 127
Church of Scotland (Education Committee), 25, 28, 74, 140, 145, 199
Class Subjects, 110, 115
Codes of Regulations, 27, 66-7, 107, 110, 111, 114, 115, 145, 151, 208, 222
Co-education, 10, 71, 125, 142, 161
Commercial Courses, 117, 118, 120, 169, 201, 211, 238
Commissions, Royal
 Argyll, 42, 55-60, 69-74
 Balfour of Burleigh, 122-6
 Colebrooke, 80-4
 Cross, 149-50
 Elgin, 216-8
 Errol, 50
 Inglis, 98-102
 Melville, 50
 Moncrieff, 85, 107-8, 121
 Newcastle, 32, 33
 Rosebery, 44-9
Commissions, Statutory
 Inglis, 86, 92-6
 Kinnear, 149-50, 158-68
Committee of Council on Education, 27, 57-8, 141-4
 Scotland, 61, 109, 234-5
 Vice-President, 31, 109
Committees, Departmental
 Craik, 205
 Elgin, 132-3
 Lushington, 182
 Mackenzie, 213-5
 Parker, 110-2, 127-30, 150
Common Good, 11, 78-9
Compulsory Attendance, 64, 108-9, 112, 117-8, 176-7, 186-7, 230-1
Craik, Sir Henry, 109, 190, 205
Cumin, Patrick, 110
Curators of Patronage (Edinburgh), 87, 101, 156

Darwin, Charles, 20
Day School Certificates, 209, 211-3, 222
Degrees
 B.A., 47, 48, 92-3, 100
 B.Com., 169
 B.D., 48, 96, 166
 B.Ed., 196
 B.L., 97, 166
 B.Sc., 96, 97, 100-1, 164-5
 Ch.M., 164
 D.D., 47, 48, 96
 D.Litt., 165, 169
 D.Phil., 165, 169
 D.Sc., 96, 97, 164, 165
 LL.B., 48, 95, 165-6
 LL.D., 47, 95
 M.A., 16, 48, 92-4, 162-3
 M.B., 95, 101, 164
 M.D., 17, 47, 48, 95, 164
 Mus.B., Mus.D., 166
 Ph.D., 169-70
Dentistry, 169, 239
Dick Bequest, 81, 145
Diplomas
 Education, 196
 L.A., 146
 L.L.A., 160-1
 Schoolmaster's, 148

Directors of Education, 219, 226, 232
Disruption, 28, 50, 92, 142
District Education Fund, 137, 179, 184
Divinity, 17, 19, 48, 166, 170-1
Dollar Academy, 38, 218
Domestic Science, 107, 114, 120, 201, 211, 235, 238
Don-Wauchope, Sir John, 62
Dumfries (proposed university), 49
Dundee High School, 40
Dundee University College, 103, 149, 151, 153, 157, 158-9, 194, 238
Dux (school), 241

Ecclesiastical History, 19
Economics, 163, 168
Edinburgh Academy, 40, 70
Edinburgh High School, 42, 70
Edinburgh University, 15, 44, 51, 87, 93, 96, 97, 146, 148, 160, 217
Education
 Adult, 186, 214, 228, 239-40
 Elementary, 23-36, 55-68, 107-20, 209, 228
 Further, 177, 186-7, 225, 228, 229, 230
 Infant, 29-30, 185, 228
 Secondary, 37-43, 69-85, 121-38, 179, 185, 209-10, 218, 221-3, 228
 Special, 175, 176, 237, 238
 Technical, 30-1, 43-4, 124, 126, 131, 211, 235, 238, 239-40
Education Authorities, 183-90, 197
Education Committees, 191
Education Department, 31, 109, 145
Education (Scotland) Fund, 178, 189, 191, 198, 204
Education, Study of, 146-8, 149, 196-7, 219, 233, 234
Educational Institute of Scotland, 206, 219, 227
Elementary Subjects, 34, 67, 114-5
Elgin Academy, 42
Endowments, Educational, 80-5, 121-6, 180-1, 213-8, 233-4
English, Study of, 14, 41, 67, 93, 110, 116, 117, 130, 136, 137, 163, 168, 177, 186, 209, 222
Episcopal Church, 39, 143-4, 152, 197-8
Equivalent Grant, 114, 132, 167, 168, 178, 191

Fearon, D. R., 70
Fees, 9, 24, 40, 41, 57, 64-5, 79, 112-4, 115, 120, 128-9, 133, 185, 198, 230
Fettes College, 76, 218
Finance, 65-6, 78-80, 85, 137-8, 178-9, 189, 191, 198
Forster, W. E., 61
Fraser, James, 69
Free Church of Scotland, 28, 51, 142, 145
Froude, J. A., 98

Gaelic, 13, 108, 110-1, 177, 185, 228
Geddes, Sir William, 89
General Aid Grant, 136, 178
Geography, 14, 41, 66, 110, 130, 211, 222
Gibson, J., 27
Gillespie's Hospital, James, 74-6
Girls, Education of, 124-5, 238
Glasgow Infant School (or Educational) Society, 30, 140
Glasgow University, 15, 89, 92, 146, 151, 154, 160-1
Glen's School, Allan, 135, 218
Gordon, J., 28
Gordon's Hospital, Robert, 82, 121
Grants, Government, 26, 34-6, 56-7, 91, 110, 112-4, 116, 128, 130-6, 158, 167, 168-9, 189, 191, 198, 240
Greek, 11, 41, 67, 93, 130
Greig, J., 56

Harvey, T., 56, 69-71
Hebrew, 17, 96, 158
Henderson, Alexander, 46
Heriot's Hospital, George, 76, 121, 123, 218
Heriot-Watt College, 43, 169
History, 41, 66, 101, 110, 130, 137, 163, 168, 209, 222
Hostels, 180, 210, 214
Huxley, T. H., 98

Inglis, John (Lord), 86, 98
Inspection, 27, 28, 66, 85, 127, 130, 233, 235-6
Intermediate Certificate, 117, 119-20, 195, 208, 212

Jex-Blake, Sophia, 160n, 161n
Johnston, Thomas, 227
Junior Leaving Certificate, 222
Junior Student System, 195, 199

Kay-Shuttleworth, Sir James, 20, 27, 30, 140-1, 143
Kerr, John, 145

Latin, 11-2, 41, 67, 93, 130, 137
Laurie, S. S., 74-5, 80, 145, 147
Law, 19, 48, 95-6, 97, 165-6
Leaving Certificate, 115, 119, 120, 127-8, 130, 135-7, 208-9, 222-3, 236, 240
Local
  Advisory Councils, 189
  Education Authorities, 190-1, 218, 228-32, 237-8, 240
  (See also Education Authorities, School Boards)
  Taxation Account, 178, 191
London University, 49, 96, 103
Loretto School, 39
Lowe, Robert, 33

Macdonald, Sir George, 190
Madras College (St. Andrews), 39, 121, 123
Magistrands, 17
Malloch, J. S., 151, 194
Mann, Horace, 31
Mathematics, 17, 41, 48, 67, 93, 127, 130, 136, 137, 211
Maxwell, C. F., 56
Medical Inspection, 176, 232
Medicine, 19-20, 48, 95, 101, 164, 239
Meiklejohn, J. M. D., 148
Melbourne, Lord, 50
Merchiston Castle School, 39
Merchant Company of Edinburgh, 75-6, 218
Merchant Maiden Hospital, 74-6
Merit Certificate, 114-5, 118, 209, 212
Milne Bequest, 81-2
Modern Languages, 41, 67, 101, 117, 130, 163, 167, 168, 200, 201
  French, 12, 14
Morgan's Hospital (Dundee), 82, 123
Mundella, A. J., 207
Music, 101, 166, 211, 235, 238

National Joint Council, 205-6, 233
Neill, A. S., 242
Newbattle Abbey, 239
Nicolson, A., 56

Owen, Robert, 29
Oxford University, 51, 96, 97, 98

Pakington, Sir John, 32
Payment by Results, 33-4, 66-7
Perth Academy, 13-4
Philosophy, 17, 48, 93, 94
Philp Bequest, 82
Physical Education, 177, 186, 201, 229, 235
Pillans, James, 41
Playfair, Lord, 98
Pneumatics, 17
Pupil-Teacher System, 143-4, 195
Qualifying Examination, 118, 208, 210, 213, 230

Queen Margaret College, 161
Queen's Scholars, 143, 145-6
Queen's Students, 151, 193
Quoad Sacra Parishes, 25, 26

Rate-Aid, 66, 214. (See also School Fund)
Rector (schools), 12, 39. (See also University)
Regents, 17-8
Religious Instruction, 63, 66, 185, 188, 191, 229, 233
Residue Grant, 113, 130, 134, 178
Revised Code, 33-5, 60
Roebuck, J. A., 26
Roman Catholic Church, 149, 152, 197
Royal Colleges, 161n, 238
  Physicians, 19
  Surgeons, 20
Royal (Dick) Veterinary College, 169
Royal Faculty of Physicians and Surgeons, 19, 239
Royal Society of Edinburgh, 20
Royal Technical College (Glasgow), 43, 169
Ruddiman, Thomas, 12
Rusk, R. R., 219

Sandford, Sir Francis, 62, 110
St. Andrews University, 15, 18, 89, 92, 93, 102-3, 148, 151, 153, 160, 238, 239
St. George's School, 125, 148, 197
St. Leonard's School, 125
School
  Boards, 62-6, 77-80, 85, 109, 138, 152, 176-80, 183
  Fund, 66, 80, 85, 126, 138, 176, 184
  Management Committees, 184
  Meals, 176, 217, 231, 235
Schools
  Academies, 14, 38, 70
  Advanced Departments, 116, 118
  Advanced Divisions, 209-11, 222
  Approved, 219-20, 235
  Assembly, 25, 56
  Burgh, 10-2, 32, 42, 63, 69-73, 77
  Day Industrial, 112, 181-2, 220
  Demonstration, 222
  Direct Grant, 238
  Endowed, 38-9, 131, 179, 180, 218, 222, 232
  English, 11
  Episcopal, 56-7, 63
  Free Church, 28, 56
  Grammar, 11, 38
  Heritors' Girls', 33
  High, 38
  Higher Class, 80, 85, 124. (See also Endowed)
  Higher Class Public, 77-80, 85, 120, 138
  Higher Grade, 116-7, 119-20, 208
  Hospitals, 73-6, 82-3, 123
  Independent, 233, 238
  Industrial, 181, 219
  Junior Colleges, 228, 231
  Mixed Burgh and Parochial, 38, 70
  Nursery, 185, 217, 228
  Omnibus, 209, 223, 240
  Organized Science, 135
  Parliamentary, 26, 56
  Parochial, 7, 10, 24, 32-3, 56, 63, 70
  Proprietary Boarding, 39
  Reformatory, 182, 219
  Roman Catholic, 56-7, 63
  Secondary (Junior, Senior), 223, 240
  Sessional, 25
  Side, 24, 56
  Spinning, 13
  S.S.P.C.K., 8, 56
  Supplementary Courses, 118, 208-9
  Voluntary, 56, 63, 184, 187-8, 191
  Writing, 13

Science, 13, 20, 31, 67, 94, 96-7, 100-1, 107-8, 117, 135, 137, 164-5, 169, 211
Science and Art Department, 31, 115, 126, 134-5
Scottish Council for Research in Education, 207, 219-20, 233
Scottish (or Scotch) Education Department, 61, 109-10, 190, 216, 217, 219-20, 235, 236-7, 240
Secondary and Technical Education Grant, 135, 178
Secondary Education Committees, 133-4, 136, 137-8, 176, 179, 181
Secretary (of State) for Scotland, 109, 154, 183, 192, 235
Selkirk High School, 218
Sellar, A. C., 56, 69-71
Semis, 17
Society for Propagating Christian Knowledge, 7-8, 12-13
Specific Subjects, 66-7, 107-8, 110, 114-5
Standard Grant, 189
Stationers' Hall, 49, 50
Stewart's Hospital, Daniel, 74-6
Stow, David, 29-30, 140-1, 142
Struthers, Sir John, 190

Tawse, 213, 241
Teachers
Certification, 144, 151, 194-5, 199-202
Pensions, 33, 65, 177-8, 203-4, 233, 234
Salaries, 5, 23, 33, 185, 204-6, 232-3
Tenure, 24, 33, 59, 65, 72, 180, 207, 222
Tertians, 17
Teviot, Lord, 206
Thomson, Sir Godfrey, 196n
Training Colleges, 30, 33, 111-2, 139-5 192,3-203, 235, 239
Training of Teachers
Central Executive Committee, 199
Committees of Management, 197, 199, 232
National Committee, 197, 198, 232
Provincial Committees, 152, 176, 193, 197, 199, 222, 232
Transfer of Schools, 63, 180, 187-8
Trinity College (Glenalmond), 39, 70

United Free Church, 152, 170
Universities, 6, 12, 14-20, 32, 44-52, 72, 86-103, 145-51, 153-71, 195-6, 238, 239, 240
University
Assistants, 166-7
Chancellor, 86, 88, 154, 158
Committee of Privy Council, 98
Scotland: 99, 154, 158, 214, 216
Court, 46, 86-7, 89-90, 98-9, 152, 153-5, 157-8, 170-1, 199
Entrance Board, 169
Entrance Examinations, 99-100, 161-2
Fees, 18, 167, 168
Franchise, 97-8, 170n
General Council, 87-8, 97-8, 99, 153-5
Grants Committee, 168
Lecturers, 101, 166-7, 170
Local Committees, 151, 193
Local Examinations, 127, 160
Ordinances, 86, 90, 92, 99, 157-8, 170
Principal, 88, 89
Professors, 17, 45, 87, 101, 155, 167, 170
Senatus Academicus, 45, 86-7, 153-5
Students' Representative Council, 156
Vice-Chancellor, 88
Ure, Andrew, 43

Veterinary Science, 169, 238, 239

Vocational Guidance, 176, 237

Watson's Hospital, George, 73-6
Women, Higher Education of, 159-61
Women Teachers, 33, 144, 145, 148-9, 197, 199-200, 201-2, 205, 233
Wood's Sessional School, John, 25, 140
Workers' Educational Association, 240

Youth Clubs, 214, 225
Youth Service, 225, 229